HOW TO **MAKE MONEY** WITH YOUR **BLOG**

The Ultimate Reference Guide for Building, Optimizing, and Monetizing Your Blog

DUANE FORRESTER AND GAVIN POWELL

New York   Chicago   San Francisco
Lisbon   London   Madrid   Mexico City   Milan
New Delhi   San Juan   Seoul   Singapore
Sydney   Toronto

The *McGraw-Hill* Companies

1 2 3 4 5 6 7 8 9 0   FGR/FGR   0 9 8 7

ISBN-13: 978-0-07-150857-5
MHID: 0-07-150857-0

McGraw-Hill books are available at special quantity discounts to use as premiums
and sales promotions, or for use in corporate training programs. For more information,
please write to the Director of Special Sales, Professional Publishing, McGraw-Hill,
Two Penn Plaza, New York, NY 10121-2298. Or contact your local bookstore.

This book is printed on acid-free paper.

I owe a debt of thanks to many people who have helped with this book. Foremost on this list is my wife, Donna—thanks for your support, Babe. It made all the difference.

Bill Hartzer is next. Thanks to Bill, I'm not just another bozo.

To Chris Sherman, Vanessa Fox, Diane Vigil, and Rose Sylvia, thanks so much for your time and thoughts on the manuscript as this project came together. It is very much appreciated.

Finally, for every single person who reads this—get blogging . . . today. You can do it, and it can pay off. It's folks just like you who really make a book like this possible, so hopefully you will get as much from it as we hope. Our plan is simple—to help *you* make money with your blog.

—DF

This is for all those bloggers out there—seeking a voice, a platform from which to show off their talents, or a place to share their enthusiasm for whatever floats their boat!

—GP

CONTENTS

PREFACE

Just to get you started, introducing this book is a simple matter of presenting you with a number of easy questions.

WHY CALL IT
HOW TO MAKE MONEY WITH YOUR BLOG?

This book is called this because you want to make money from your blog. That is why you are reading this book. The original title was *Making Money with Blogging.* It was then changed to *Power Blogging for Bucks,* and finally this name was chosen as the most obvious, concise, and appropriate for the content of this book.

Can blogging help you to make money? Absolutely! Search engines and their automated search bots just love blogs. This means that with a few simple techniques, you can have a blog that ranks well for selected phrases and gains exposure for you through search engines like Google, Yahoo, and MSN. In other words, blogs and blog entries can be listed, and even listed automatically, once they have been set up. Bloggers are generally seen as some of the most cutting-edge content creators online today. They harness the real power of blogging, stating their opinions in a free-speech-type environment.

> Note: *Free speech* is a loosely applied term. For example, creating a blog with a blog service provider requires that one abide by their rules. If you don't comply, an Internet Service Provider (ISP) can inhibit your page views, your advertising revenue, and even delete your blog.

People who write blogs are often extremely driven, creative, independent, and successful individuals. These types of people want to know how they can utilize their blogs to the limit and earn money in the process.

WHO ARE THE AUTHORS OF
HOW TO MAKE MONEY WITH YOUR BLOG?

The two authors of this book are Duane Forrester and Gavin Powell.

Duane Forrester is a leading expert in his field of online marketing, search engine optimization and blogging. Duane owns and administers numerous Web sites and blogs. Because his blogs make money through advertising, they accomplish just what this book is about: making money with blogs and blogging. Duane also frequently makes presentations all over North America. Duane can be contacted at the following e-mail address:

- duane@theonlinemarketingguy.com

Duane runs the following blogs and Web sites:

- www.theonlinemarketingguy.com

- www.ajeepthing.com/jeep-blog

- www.blowupmyride.com

- www.dieseldiesel.com

- www.weirdnewsbits.com

In addition to running his own blogs, Duane is an SEO Manager with the Microsoft Corporation. He volunteers as a moderator at www.searchengineforums.com and can be found posting in numerous other spaces online as SportsGuy. He also volunteers as a member of the board of directors at SEMPO.org and cochairs its in-house

SEM Committee. Duane even finds time to write articles for leading search marketing Web sites such as www.searchenginewatch.com and www.searchengineland.com.

Gavin Powell is an experienced computer technical writer with numerous titles in print, a software developer and administrator, and a semiprofessional composer and musician. Gavin also owns and administers various Web sites and blogs. Gavin can be contacted at the following e-mail addresses:

- ezpowell@ezpowell.com

- oracledba@oracledbaexpert.com

Gavin runs the following blogs and Web sites:

- http://ezpowellmusic.blogspot.com

- www.myspace.com/ezpowell

- www.youtube.com/ezpowell

- www.ezpowell.com

- www.oracledbaexpert.com

CHAPTER SUMMARY

Each chapter covers a specific area of *How to Make Money with Your Blog* and making money with your blog:

- *Chapter 1. "Quick Starts: Top 10 Lists."* This is an effective and efficient way to kick off this book, particularly because *How to Make Money with Your Blog* is a business-technical title. A list of dos and don'ts at the beginning of this book gives you something to work with right off the bat. And it's all directly from an expert blogger.

- *Chapter 2. "Blogs and Search Optimization (SEO)."* This chapter is all about telling you things that will help you as a revenue-producing blogger before you even begin as a blogger. Search engines just love blogs, which is good for the art of *How to Make Money with Your Blog.* Some simple techniques can improve your blog ranking for selected phrases in search engines and gain good exposure for you. You need to know about templates (blog providers) and their different capabilities. You also need to know about where and how your blog postings will be stored. You need to understand how to use keywords to enable you to write your blog postings in a manner that makes them big, fat, juicy targets for search engines to find. You will also find some dedicated SEO tips for blogs in here. Essentially, you need to know how to structure and write articles so that people will read them, click on your ads, and ultimately generate some advertising revenue for you.

- *Chapter 3. "Generating Revenue with Your Blog."* How long will it take you to make money with your content and your blog? Building a blog with great content and getting it to rank well is one thing. If you've done the building and optimizing correctly, you'll see traffic increase and page views start to climb. Of course, as with any business venture, there's no way to make easy money. You have to be patient, positive, and persistent. Having a blog and seeing it make money takes work and an investment of time. Be prepared to run through several months of updating content, not generating much revenue to begin with.

- *Chapter 4. "Managing Your Blog."* What should you as a blogger be doing on a daily basis to keep your blog up and running? You need to keep your blog as available and visible as possible and make as much advertising revenue as you can get. That's an ideal, but it's a good goal to aim for. That goal is realistic if you are patient and don't expect to make millions. A few of the tasks involved in managing your blog are controlling spam and treating your blog like a business (even if it's a fun business)—especially if you expect to make revenue to cover more than a cup of coffee. Most important are feeds that allow you to automatically get repeat visitors back to your blog in the future. If your blog is interesting and useful enough, then readers will subscribe. You need to provide the facility for readers to subscribe by providing them with an online feed.

- *Chapter 5. "Extras and Inspiration."* This chapter consists of a few small loose ends that can't be left out, but don't fit well elsewhere. Blogging is all about communication. That communication is all typed on a computer keyboard, but the basic principle of winning friends and influencing people still applies. This chapter also gives you some general comments and advice on how to be successful as a blogger and how to, or how not to, tap into the power and reach of leading blogs and blogging platforms such as MySpace. There is also a review of up-and-coming technology such as audioblogging and videoblogging.

With that, let's get started with how you, the reader, can make money out of your blog (or blogs). Let's get to *How to Make Money with Your Blog!*

HOW TO **MAKE MONEY** WITH YOUR **BLOG**

QUICK STARTS: **TOP 10** LISTS

One way to kick off a book like this is to cut right to the chase and give you some simple, straightforward, top 10 lists of dos and don'ts. So, without further ado, let's get to it.

10 STEPS TO BLOGGING REVENUE

The objective is to make your blog successful—as a source of advertising revenue, as a way to gain some exposure for yourself, as a way to state your case, or as a combination of all three. This book focuses more on the blogonomical side of blogging. So, fortune rather than fame is the primary focus of this book.

You can employ these 10 steps to help make your blog a roaring success:

1. *Code access.* Ensure the platform allows access to the code so you can place items in the order you choose. Otherwise, you may not be able to rearrange the things on your blog pages the way that you want them.

2. *Keyword research.* Do your keyword research to select the best keywords to use to integrate into your blog titles, your blog name, article titles, and so on.

3. *Categories and keywords.* Edit your categories to integrate keywords into URLs.

4. *Linking to other blogs.* Add links to other blogs. A few related blogs is more than adequate, but make sure they are useful to your readers and that those links are trustworthy. Trust is a big issue for people using the Internet.

5. *Importance of blog directory submissions.* Get your blog into the top blog directories; you want the links from those directories back to your blog. This is very important because it will give your blog better visibility. People can find you more easily.

6. *Regular directory submissions.* Submit to the usual directories, including Google, Yahoo, and DMOZ.org. This is especially important if your blog is also your Web site.

7. *Blog posting length.* A *blog* is an entity into which you make entries (post your written articles). Each entry or article is called a *post,* a *posting,* or an *article.* Try for post lengths of at least 200 words, and integrate selected keywords near

the top of the post. The keyword should be related to the title and is used by search engines to help understand the focus of the article.

8. *Moderating your blog.* Be alert for comment spam. Moderate all comments and delete those containing useless links, those that are off topic, any adult-related items, or anything that might offend your readers.

9. *Clean URLs.* Use clean URLs if the option is given. A clean URL hides many of the operators and coding characters. Clean URLs are easier for a search engine spider to crawl and index into its related search engine automatically.

10. *Frequency of new blog postings.* Make frequent postings. Although it is not Search Engine Optimization (SEO) per se, frequent posts will keep the spiders coming back to see what's new. This will help to keep fresh content flowing into search engine indexes from your domain.

10 THINGS TO AVOID WHEN BLOGGING

Ideally, you will want to make a concerted effort to avoid practices that are not sensible from a blogonomical perspective. Generally, be as honest and objective as possible without being overly opinionated. In other words, be honest without being offensive. Stick to the topic with a positive approach by offering solutions, rather than pointing out negative issues with no possible solutions. When it comes to opinions, let your readers and commenters offer their opinions, but watch to ensure everyone is being given an equal voice, which is free from ridicule. Contributing commenters should feel free to express their own opinions on topics, but keep in mind that if those opinions clash with the best interests of advertisers, you could have problems.

Employ these 10 steps to help you avoid a disastrous blog:

1. *Credibility killers.* If you take products for review make sure that you disclose this to your readers. Be honest. Also, when placing advertisements on your blog, be very careful in choosing advertisers whose products or services are topically relevant.

2. *Lack of activity.* Make regular postings as often as a few times a week, perhaps even once a day. Posting once a month or once a year is pointless. Also, making seven posts all at once, once per week, is ineffective in comparison to doing a single post per a day. If you write seven posts all at once—store them locally on your computer and then post them one at a time over the next seven days. Give your readers a chance to read each posting.

3. *Lack of content.* Avoid postings that are very short. Generally, 200 words is a good length. Anything longer might be scanned too quickly or avoided for being too much to read. And a 10-word entry may be seen as not offering any value. Remember, your readers are spending their precious time reading your blog, as much as you are spending your precious time writing it.

4. *Hot linked images.* Hot linking most often refers to the practice of inserting an image into your article that is hosted by another Web site. Basically, you're using their image and bandwidth without permission. Hot linking is also known as *inline linking, leaching, direct linking,* or *bandwidth theft.* With all those derogatory terms, it should suffice to say that hot linking is not a fair practice.

5. *Advertising overload.* While it may seem tempting to sign up for multiple ad programs and use the maximum number of allowable ads from each program on your blog, this is a surefire recipe for failure. Too many ads will chase

readers away and detract from the content of your blog. If you decide to use ads from multiple programs, read their rules carefully and be judicious in your placement of ad units. Less is often more.

6. *Duplicating content of others.* Copying and pasting without permission or without credit could lead to a bad reputation for you. Also, be aware that deliberate copyright infringement can render you liable, which can cost more than you might imagine. Also, in the United States and elsewhere, infringing on someone else's copyright can leave you subject to criminal prosecution.

7. *Offensive postings.* Certain postings may offend readers, advertisers, or other bloggers. Yes, the Internet does have a spirit of free speech and free enterprise, but if you are trying to make money, avoid commentary that could cause offense. Some blog providers allow readers to mark a blog as being offensive. Enough negative flagging can get you switched off. Then you have to start all over again elsewhere. That's not effective use of your time.

8. *Maintaining objectivity.* Don't stray off the topic of your blog or your posting. For example, if your blog is about Jeeps, then don't spend time talking about Ferraris— unless, of course, that topic is somehow relevant to Jeeps. Focus on the point of your blog and your postings. Don't avoid topics and content that may make advertisers look a little silly. However, in the long run it is sometimes better to absorb a little friction with an advertiser than to risk losing readers. It is up to advertisers to answer for their products, not you. You are not there to specifically sell products for someone else—you are merely telling people what they can buy and where to find it. If certain advertisers have product issues, it is better for their business to attend to those issues that their customers may be com-

plaining about on your blog. In short, it is better for an advertiser to respond to a small problem rather than find out about a problem when it's big enough to hurt them.

9. *Comment spam.* You need to police your comments for spam. Captchya code entries can be used for open entry comment fields.

Note: A captchya code is an image with letters and numbers shown to the reader. The image can usually be read only by the human eye; most spiders cannot read the text in the image, thus precluding them from posting automated spam comments.

Switching off trackbacks can also help to reduce comment spam.

Note: A *trackback* is a little like a remote comment, where the comment is not directly posted to your blog, but rather posted to the commenter's blog and then pinged back to yours. As a result, trackbacks are subjected to much automation and are thus comment spam.

10. *Poorly designed templates.* Ugly templates that make you squint, squirm, and wriggle in your seat, or that look just odd or ugly—should just be avoided. Try to blend both foreground and background colors of your blog and ads. The more discernible the contrast between advertisement and blog, the less likely it will get clicked on.

BLOGS AND SEARCH ENGINE **OPTIMIZATION** (SEO)

WHAT'S IN THIS CHAPTER?

This chapter is all about telling you things that will help you as a revenue-producing blogger before you even start blogging.

Search engines love blogs. This is a good thing for you. It means with simple techniques, you can have a blog that ranks well for selected phrases and gains added exposure for you. If you choose to operate only a blog, that's fine. If you choose to run a blog along with an actual Web site, that's fine again. If you choose to operate your blog as your Web site, that's also fine.

Before you go out and grab yourself an account with blogger .com, there are some things you'll need to know. All of the basic tenets of search optimization that apply to Web sites also apply to blogs. So the basic SEO knowledge you're building will be useful even if you choose only to run a stand-alone blog.

Before you start, you need to know such things as which platforms you might choose to use and how each platform gives you different capabilities. You also need to know about where and how your blog postings will be stored. You need to understand how to use keywords, so that you write your blog postings in a manner that makes them big, fat, juicy targets for search engines to find. Essentially, you need to know how to structure and write articles so that people will read them, click on your ads, and ultimately generate some advertising revenue for you.

THE POWER OF BLOGS

Bloggers are generally seen as some of the most cutting-edge content creators online today. They state their opinions and say it like it is—that's the real power of the medium. Its ability to allow individuals to express themselves worldwide, almost instantly, is also part of its power.

When optimized well and submitted to leading blog directories, it's completely possible to have multiple references to your own blog on a page of search results for the targeted phrase.

For a long time, blogs were seen as nothing more than an online diary: a space where people could voice their opinions, raise their voices, or post anything that struck them as interesting. The key was the ease with which blogs could be started.

You needed no knowledge of coding or Web design. You

needed to know nothing of usability or layout. You simply needed to know what you liked and how to navigate online in general. Many sources, such as Blogger.com catered to this market with an intuitive, user-friendly interface designed to help anyone start his or her own blog in minutes.

And start they did—thousands a week seemed to suddenly appear. Everyone had a voice. But was anyone reading?

Given that blogs were not immediately started en masse by businesses, but rather by everyday people, it took time for the concept to take hold in mainstream business. In the early days, if you stumbled onto a blog that you liked, you'd just bookmark it and return when you felt like it.

Today is a very different world for blogging, though seemingly very little time has passed since blogs first began to grow in numbers.

Today, your business is out of date if it doesn't offer a blog. If you're a professional and not keeping a blog, others wonder why. And if you're looking to start a business online, blogs offer one of the cheapest, quickest, and easiest to use methods of gaining a Web presence.

All the basics still apply:

- They're easy to set up.

- They are completely customizable.

- There are thousands of themes available to suit any look, layout, or feel.

- Prices run from free to whatever your budget can afford.

Blogs have evolved into legitimate Web sites on their own. Given the platforms that run them, many businesses choose blogs as the basis for all their Web-based content. It makes it easy to update the look and feel when redesigning, and it's supersimple to add new pages of content, new products, or entire sections to the site.

Indeed, the terms *blog, site,* and *Web site* may well be used interchangeably . . . though, while every blog can be called a Web site, not every Web site is a blog.

Blogs are so prevalent today that even the biggest companies operate them, sometimes several each. Google has many blogs, both official and unofficial. Yahoo is the same. What about MSN? Yep. How about General Motors, Ford, and most of the auto manufacturers? Yep, though mostly targeting the press, they are there. CNN and pretty much every other major news source operate a series of blogs—often tied to segments of news or to TV anchors and personalities.

Blogs are allowing real-time reporting from areas of the world in conflict; they allow soldiers to keep family up-to-date, and they allow people to share knowledge and expertise globally. Blogs have the power to educate and entertain. They also have the power to generate revenue.

Blogs represent an easy way to quickly disseminate news and information to a mass readership. They are a way to segment information and thus to segment your readers. Here's an example of the blogging world's ability to spread information fast and far.

Jennifer Laycock is a great gal. She runs her own online business (www.searchengineguide.com), and when she became a new mom, she felt strongly enough about breast-feeding and its benefits to start her own site dedicated to it (www.thelactivist.com). She sells some T-shirts and other items (the Milk Bank Line) with catchy slogans on them, and 100 percent of the proceeds from this line go to help the Mother's Milk Bank in Ohio near her home. Additionally, she donates 10 percent of all other sales as well—about $2,000 to date.

Being creative, one brainstorming session led Jen to the slogan "Breast: The Other White Milk." It's a play on a well-known slogan, so it's funny and coy at the same time.

Little did Jen know the issues this would raise. The National Pork Board, having created the original slogan, "Pork: The Other

White Meat," issued a tough-stance letter to Jen ordering her to cease the use of her slogan or face legal action.

This was not what she had expected when she started out on this path. In fact, the whole thing seemed a bit heavy-handed and sudden. A large national board representing a known product was going to hunt down a small business owner and new mom, to take legal action over a slogan being used to support a local nonprofit. It seemed, many felt, a bit much. Sure, the pork producers had to protect their copyrights, but where was the warning? Where was the e-mail or phone call asking her to stop? Why jump straight to legal action?

The day Jen posted about this on her blog, the insider network lit up. Hundreds of bloggers, influencing thousands of readers, ran with the story. It exploded across North America via the underground network of news sources—synonymous with blogging.

One item contained in many posts was a request for readers to contact the National Pork Board to express their opinion about the situation.

Within days, Jen had received an apology, had discussed the situation, and had agreed to change her slogan (she never disputed the board's claim to the original or that hers was a takeoff on it); and from the top down, as members of the National Pork Board learned why Jen was selling the shirts, employees dug deep and donated money to the Mother's Milk Bank in Ohio. Because the National Pork Board as a legal entity was unable to donate, the employees took it upon themselves to offer support.

This example is a clear indicator of the reach and power of blogs. There was never any malice intended by the National Pork Board in this incident, which had no personal issues with Jen. It was simply a matter of the board's policing what it owned—and maybe of a slightly overzealous employee. Not the end of the world for anyone, but it showed in crystal clarity how quickly blogs are capable of spreading news and galvanizing readers to respond to something.

The bottom line comes down to community. Build a solid community and your blog will thrive and revenue will be positive. Abuse this community or neglect your readers and they will respond by choosing another source to read.

✦

BASELINE: WHAT PLATFORM TO USE

There are several options to choose from when looking for a blogging platform. They range from free platforms to paid-for platforms, from fully supported to completely unsupported. In this section you can read about some of the more popular blogging platform options.

Blogger

Blogger is run by Google and is a decent, free, and fully supported option—found at www.blogger.com. While Blogger has limits such as not allowing complete access to all the metadata, it's very easy to set up and maintain.

> Note: The metadata being referenced here is basically the <title>, <meta description>, and <meta keyword> "tags" commonly found by viewing the source code of a page (right-click>>view source). It appears at the top of the coding, usually, and helps explain to the search engines what the content on the page is about. It's important to be able to edit at least the <title> and <description> "tags."

In addition, Blogger is fully supported, so you never have to worry about coding and databases. Blogger will allow you to place Google AdSense ads into your blog, provided that you have an AdSense account. AdSense is perfect for generating revenue from blog traffic, which is something we'll cover more later on. Blogger also now supports third-party ad codes. Now you can take ads from just about any advertising network and place them in a blog on this platform.

Figure 2.1 shows the blog creation screen for the Blogger platform template.

Note: This book contains screen shots of Web sites on the Internet. These screen shots were all taken as this book was being written. Things might have changed—a lot! The screens you see in your browser could be very different, but it is probable that the meaning will be the same. Screen shots are included so that you can read this book without having to sit at your computer at the same time.

FIGURE 2.1: GOOGLE'S BLOGGER BLOG CREATION SCREEN.

The beauty of Blogger is that it provides very easy access to the world of blogs for computer novices who know nothing about how all that stuff on their computer works. You really can create a Blogger account in three easy steps. As shown in Figure 2.1, those three easy steps are as follows:

1. Create an account.

2. Name your blog.

3. Choose a template.

You can go through those steps now if you want, and create your first blog by following this simple sequence:

1. As shown in Figure 2.1, click the big arrow button called CREATE YOUR BLOG NOW. On your computer the button should be orange.

2. The next screen allows you to create a Blogger account. Various details have been entered, as shown in Figure 2.2. The only points to note are that you must use an existing e-mail address (yours). A captchya code is also required. Otherwise, if you make mistakes the screen will tell you and you can correct any errors.

3. Scroll down and you'll find another one of those pretty-looking orange arrow buttons (black arrow button in the printed version of this book). The arrow button says, CONTINUE on it. Click that continue button. (See Figure 2.3.)

Note: An Internet address is a name for a location on the Internet. It is also known as a Universal Resource Locator (URL). Don't ask why on that one—it just is. The location of an Internet address is physically routed to electronically, using a coded address called an Internet Protocol (IP) address. That IP address is a sequence of four 3-digit num-

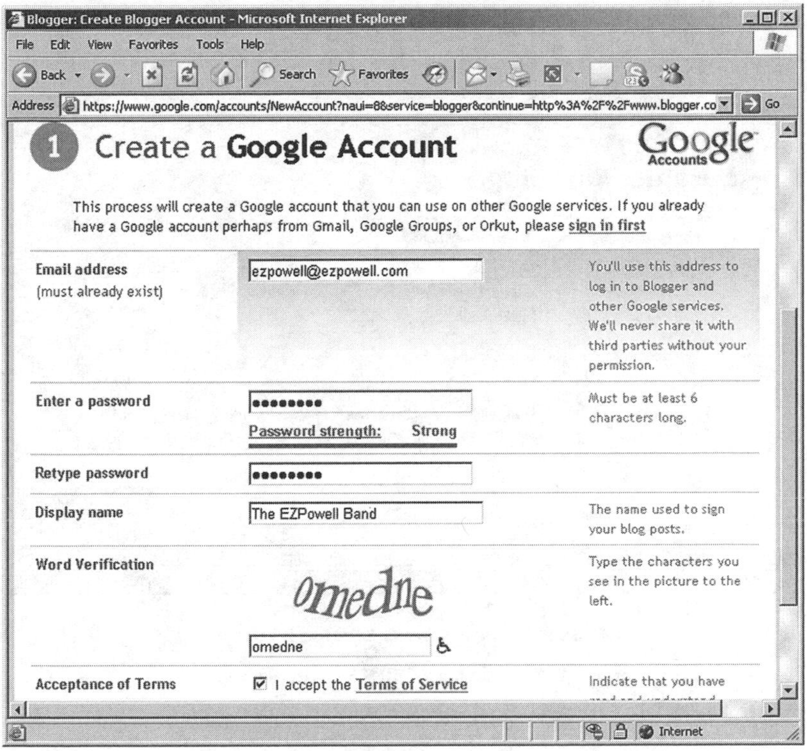

FIGURE 2.2: CREATING A BLOGGER ACCOUNT.

bers separated by periods. For example, 67.139.134.231 is the IP address for Gavin's band's Web site, whose name is www.ezpowell.com. That name is called a Directory Name Service (DNS) name. The DNS name is the thing you type into your browser. Special computers, called DNS computers, store the matching names and IP addresses. The Internet constantly uses those DNS computers to look up an IP address every time an Internet name (DNS name) is typed into a browser—somewhere out there in cyberspace.

4. The next step is to choose a template, as shown in Figure 2.4.

**FIGURE 2.3: NAMING YOUR BLOG AND
GIVING IT AN INTERNET ADDRESS.**

5. I changed my selection from the top left template to the top right template—just to see what it looks like. You can preview each template when selecting, as shown by the preview-template link below each template. Click the CONTINUE button arrow to keep going. You'll get a new window telling you that you have created a blog.

6. Click the START POSTING button to start posting articles to your blog.

7. Figure 2.5 shows the next screen, and I have created a new posting as well. And just as important as the posting text itself, I have added both a title (the Title entry at top left) and labels (the Label entry at bottom right). Title and label entries are the perfect places to integrate keywords for which you'd like to be found. Search engines use these keywords to help understand the topic of the post, and

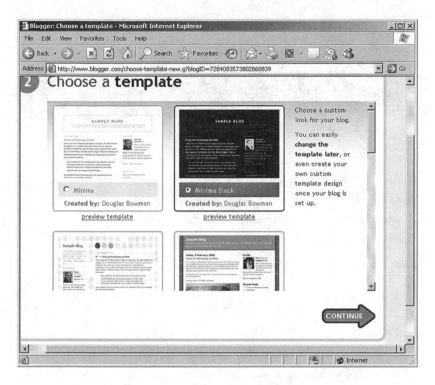

FIGURE 2.4: SELECTING A BLOGGER TEMPLATE
IS AS EASY AS CLICK AND CLICK.

along with many other factors, the engines then rank pages in order. Getting this combination right can result in an effective ranking and generating lots of traffic from people searching for your topic.

8. You can now click the PUBLISH POST button at bottom left to put your stuff out there.

9. One other thing for you to see and understand is what is meant by a blog template. Click the Back button after having published your posting. Then click the Template link found toward the top middle of the screen, as shown in Figure 2.5. You get the screen shown in Figure 2.6. Templates allow you to add, subtract, and arrange elements.

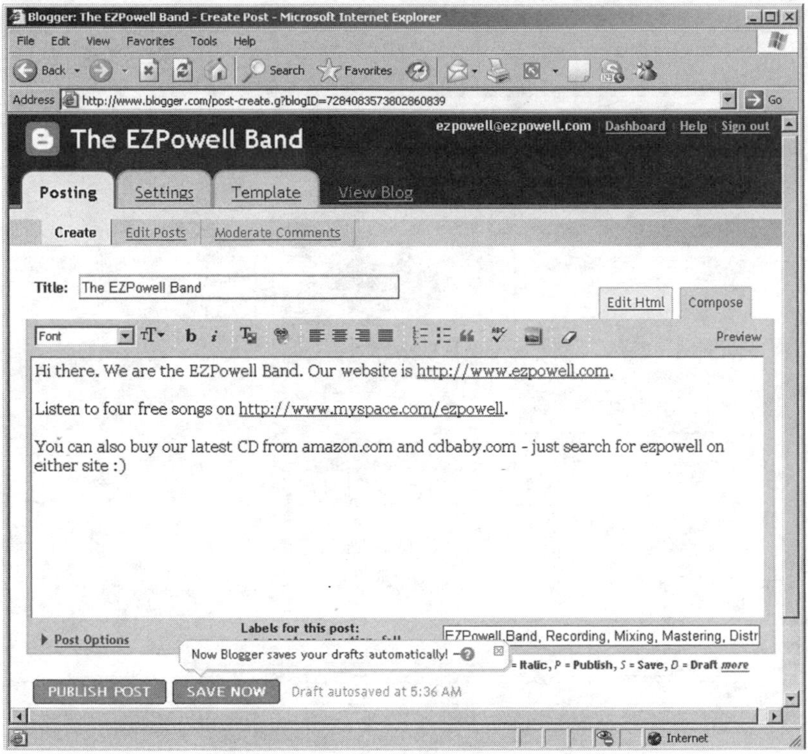

**FIGURE 2.5: CREATING A NEW POSTING
ON BLOGGER IS JUST TYPING.**

10. Figure 2.6 shows that you can arrange and rearrange your blog elements. Figure 2.7 shows some of the variety of elements you can add to your blog when clicking Add a Page Element links, as shown in Figure 2.6.

That was easy wasn't it? Anyone can do that, really. The only thing you have not so far seen is the blog you just created. You can view your newly created blog by clicking on Preview or View buttons, depending on where in Blogger you are, or even just by typing your blog URL into a browser window. The preceding blog I have just created is seen in Figure 2.8, which shows the black background of the nondefault template I chose back in Figure 2.4.

So, what's the point? It is really, really easy to get a blog up and

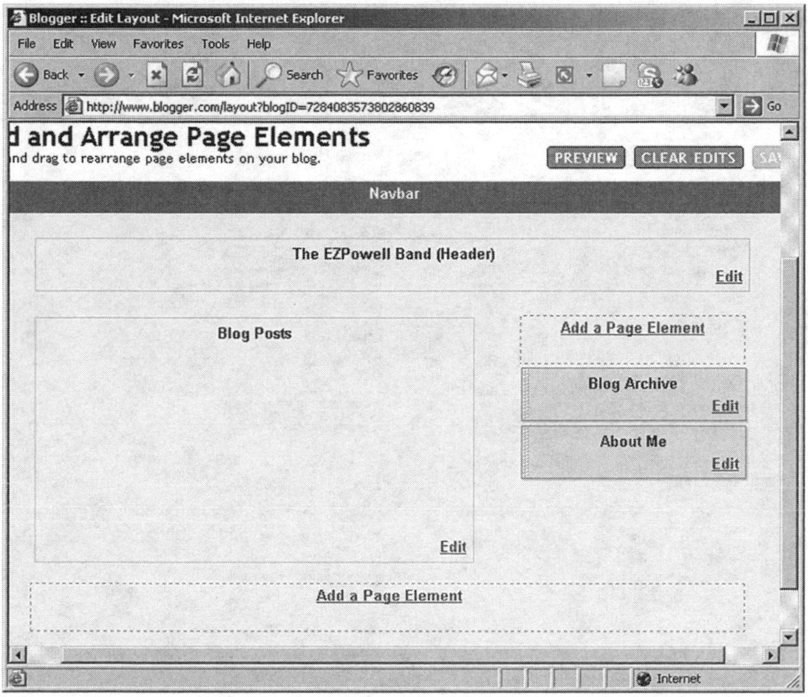

FIGURE 2.6: CHANGING TEMPLATE ELEMENTS ON BLOGGER.

running on the Internet. There is much, much more to it than that, but it's a great start, don't you think?

Open Source Blog Platforms

If you want more direct control over the appearance of your blog, its layout, structure, and features—then an open-source platform might be just the ticket. By their very nature, open-source items are free to everyone. The drawback is that they are rarely built by professional businesses and often have limited direct support. Open-source items tend to be built by very talented folks who are excellent programmers. They may, in fact, be professional programmers by day, but for the most part they build open-source items on their own time.

This simply means you'll have to rely on community-based

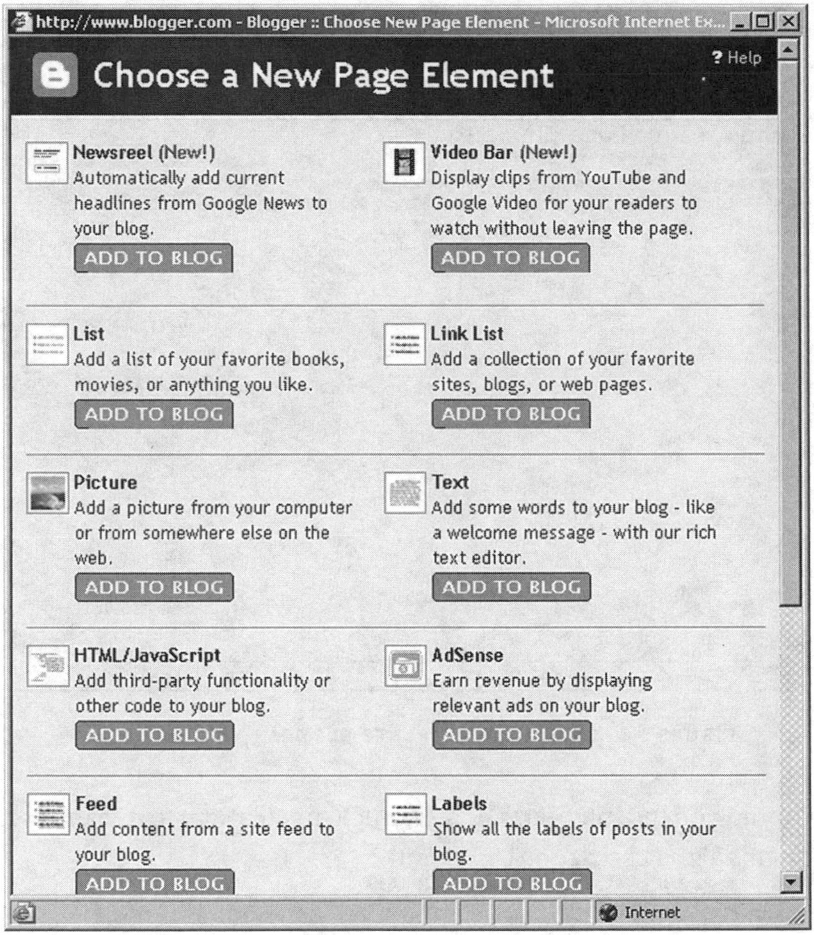

FIGURE 2.7: TYPES OF BLOGGER TEMPLATE ELEMENTS.

posting forums to ask questions about your platform. It's a good idea to have some understanding of how to work with code before you start playing with your open-source blog, as there's no quick, easy reset button if you muck things up.

Okay, you've been scared enough about open-source options, but they remain the best way to build your blog. To that end, here are a couple of solid places to start. These recommendations come from Duane's experience using these platforms, while other recommended options may be seen in the list that follows.

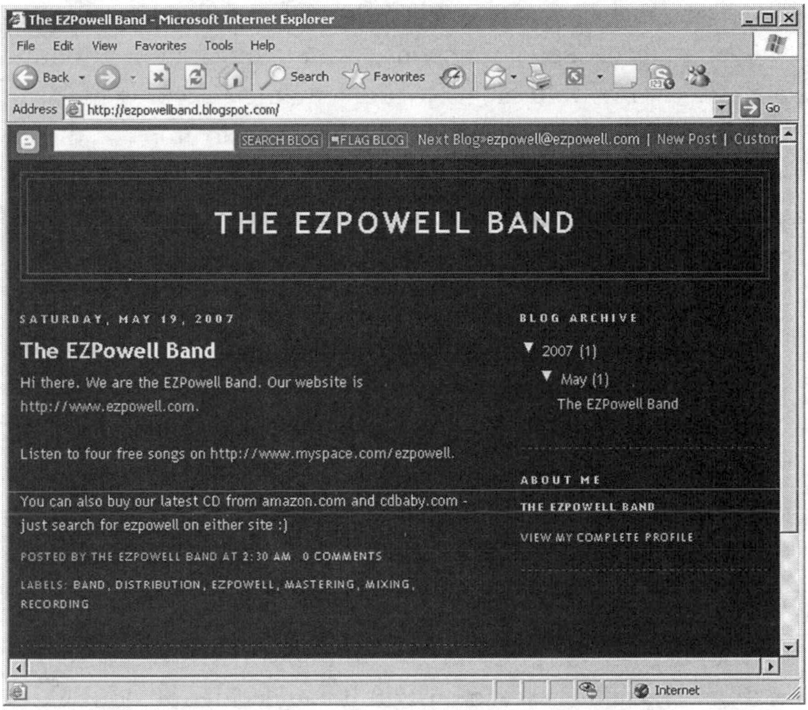

FIGURE 2.8: DISPLAYING A BLOGGER BLOG IN YOUR BROWSER.

WORDPRESS

WordPress (www.wordpress.org) is one of the leading blog platforms used today. In fact, its ability to run a blog is only one portion of what the WordPress platform is capable of. It's what's known as a *Content Management System* (CMS). Its job is to take data you provide to it, store that data, and then show it later inside whatever template you tell it to. Blogs just happen to be one form of template.

There is a massive WordPress community to help with everything from install issues to even the most dramatic coding snafus. One of its claims to fame is *The Famous 5 Minute Install.* This is no exaggeration—the install can indeed be done in about five minutes, provided you've done the database setup work beforehand.

This platform also enjoys a tremendous amount of support

from users. WordPress uses neat little devices called *plug-ins* to allow it to perform special functions. Want to integrate your online photo gallery into your blog? No problem, there's a plug-in. Want to translate your blog into different languages? No problem, there's a plug-in. Want to quickly and easily integrate ads? Again, there's a plug-in. The plug-ins are easy to install by following these simple steps:

1. Download the file to your computer.

2. Open your server to the www.domain.com/wp-contents/ plugins folder.

3. Copy the file into the folder.

4. Go back to the blog, enter the Admin/Plugins section.

5. Click the plug in to activate it.

The coding is all done for you, everything works as advertised (in most cases), and it's easy to turn off if you decide you don't like it down the road.

WordPress offers hosted versions and a stand-alone version that requires you to provide a server to run things on. Be sure to read the requirements documentation, though, as the newer versions of WordPress play nice only with newer versions of the required software (PHP, MySQL database, etc.) when they are already installed on your server.

Running a WordPress-based blog on your own will require a place to host it (on a server computer). You will need access to the files on the server, as well as access to set up a database.

Note: The term *access* implies that you need security access to be able to both read and write files. To set up a server yourself, you might have to talk to an administrator for whomever rents you server space. The latter might be complicated.

To those new to the process, the WordPress installation instructions are spot-on and will have you live in an afternoon if you follow them carefully. While the WordPress platform itself is free to download and use, you will need server space on which to host it, and that will cost you. How much depends on where you get your services, but expect it to range from around $10 per month to more than $100 per month, depending on the level of service you require.

BBlog

BBlog (www.bBlog.com) can wholeheartedly be recommended as well. Its platform is stable and easy to use. It can also be a learning experience, especially if you are not a *sysadmin* (systems administrator—a person who looks after servers) or programmer by day. Many things will be new, and you're on your own to learn the ins and outs of all this stuff. BBlog's biggest past issue has been a feature called *trackbacks*. Most blog platforms offer this, but older versions of BBlog had some real issues that led to spam. Trackbacks are simply the URLs for each article you post. Trouble is, they are visible on the bottom of each post, and when found by spiders scraping sites for URLs to spam, you may end up with thousands of spam comments to moderate each day. There is a simple fix for the problem. So don't let this deter you from exploring this option. The moderating process is made easier by allowing you to "bulk-moderate" comments. So it's relatively quick to select multiple comments and click delete to remove them. Newer versions of BBlog have login processes that help cut down on the ability of spiders to post spam comments, greatly reducing this headache (i.e., getting lots of spam).

There is an active support community for BBlog (pronounced "bee-blog"), so you do have somewhere to turn when you need help. It takes time to get the answers, but the folks there try their best to help when they can . . . and it's free. It's tough to fault it, really.

SIXAPART

Sixapart, at www.sixapart.com, offers its Typepad and Moveable Type platforms and is another strong blogging option, though it is not free. Typically, Sixapart costs run from about $50 per year for a basic Typepad Blog up to more than $200 for the Moveable Type options. Which one is best for you will depend on the level of access you need and the number of blogs you intend to operate.

A further alternative is a hosted option run through an agreement with outside hosting companies—more information can be found at www.sixapart.com/typepad/pricing. These packages vary in price and support, but for a few dollars a month you can be up and running in no time.

Sixapart offers an installation service, and if you're set on its products, it might be worth paying the fee for it. Be careful when getting Sixapart products set up by its installation service. Be honest about your level of knowledge when it comes to managing a server, as certain things will need to be done on the server before Sixapart can install the blog software/platform for you. It can be a frustrating challenge to try to learn as you go, though even a modest amount of exposure to servers and how they operate can eliminate most of the drama from the process.

OTHER OPENSOURCE PLATFORMS

Here are some other options you can explore—they are a mix of free and paid-for options:

- Greymatter (www.noahgrey.com/greysoft)

- Live Journal (www.livejournal.com)

- 20Six UK (www.20six.co.uk)

- MindSay (www.mindsay.com)

- Drupal (www.drupal.org)

In addition, an almost limitless number of companies offer free or paid blogs as stand-alone Web sites. Almost every hosting provider now offers blogs to clients, but beware that many will offer you a free blog only to control the ad spaces themselves. If you intend to make money with your blog, watch carefully for these and avoid them. GoDaddy.com offers a free blog system like this. It will do everything for you, but its ads will always be visible on your site, and, in fact, they are quite obtrusive.

If you select a platform such as WordPress, most of your work is done for you. We're big fans of this platform and we use it ourselves.

Hosting Issues

Hosting, simply put, is how and where your blog is stored—its pages, images, videos, and so on. You must have a server hosting your data for the blog to be live and for users to see, find, and read your blog on the Internet.

Hosting options range from hosting yourself on your own PC to renting and/or buying a dedicated server just for yourself. The cost of these options may fall in the category of "you're already paying for it as part of your Internet connection at home," or you may be asked to pay thousands of dollars up front, and perhaps even hundreds more per month.

Time to get real here, too—do you really need to spend $100 a month on a dedicated server for your blog? Is your blog so sought after that the instant it goes live it will have thousands of people visiting it every day?

I'm pretty sure the answers to both of those questions are no. You might wish the answers were different, and given time and hard work they may *become* different. Let's be realistic for now. Starting off, your blog won't take up much space, and there won't be thousands of people there each day to begin with.

Let's take a more detailed look at typical hosting options:

- *Do-it-yourself.* While this option exists, it's pretty limiting. Sure, you could put the gear on your PC or on your own server, but then users are limited to *your* connection speed at home, and the site won't be live if you turn off your computer each night. Let's skip this option completely— it's not a viable option if your goal is to operate your blog as a business.

- *Hosted template blog.* Generally, this is a cheap way to get a functioning, attractive blog live in one evening—great if you are just starting off, want a free way to begin, and are not concerned that others may be using the same template. Templates mean you drag and drop your pictures where you want them, there's no coding involved, and you typically get a selection to choose from. The trouble is as follows:

  Other blogs exist that are virtually identical to your blog because a template is used.

  You often have very little control over changing meta-tag data, as you most likely will not be able to access the code. You may be able to enter a description and suggest keywords, but these "tags" will be repetitively placed on every page of your site—not the best option, but workable.

- *Virtual dedicated server.* This option gives you control over your own "virtual" server. The added benefit here is you get to control your section of the server: you install what you like on it, set up users, domains, and subdomains, tweak folder structures, and, in some cases, your interface allows you to edit documents right there on the server—no copying them to your PC, updating, saving and re-uploading to refresh things or make simple changes.

  You will also have the choice of being hosted in a Windows environment or in a Linux environment. Please choose the Linux environment. Chances are you're fairly new as a Webmaster, and, trust us, adding system administration (sysadmin) to the docket will be a hefty weight. Learning how to do things in the Linux environment isn't that different than in Windows; it's simply that many simple things you'll want to do later can be controlled very easily through editing one document in a Linux environment. One real bonus to Linux-based hosting is its compatibility with the .php language. This is important if you ever want to use anything from the open-source community—such as other blog software or posting forum applications. Open-source items don't work well with Windows hosting, and sometimes not at all.

- *Dedicated hosting*. This one is simple: the whole server is yours. You are the only one using it; you maintain it; the space and capacity are all yours—everything is you. The trouble is, it's expensive—often more than $100 per month. This is not really what most folks starting out need.

The most critical component of all this is the database. It's where your blog will live. It's where all your posts are stored, where user comments are kept, and where everything from passwords to user IP addresses will end up. Make sure you have a database that is compatible with whatever blog platform you choose to use. Most blog platforms will require a MySQL database, so it'll be almost mandatory that you use a Linux-based server to accommodate this requirement. Windows-based servers use Microsoft SQL Server databases and many blog platforms simply won't work with SQL Server and Windows. If you decide to use a Windows server, look into something called Community Server for Windows servers. It will allow you to run blogs (and other things). It's not the easiest tool to work with, but is stable and relatively quick to implement.

IP Addresses: Dedicated versus Shared

This is less of a concern today than it was even just a year ago. It's still something that we recommend people look into, though.

When you choose a hosting option, the default is to run your Web site on a shared IP address. Your IP address might be 123.123.123.12, and you might learn that others have the same IP address. This does not mean users will go to someone else's Web site; it simply means that the numerical address used to "locate" your Web site by spiders and so on, is the same as another Web site.

Normally this type of thing isn't a big concern, but if the last person to use that IP address was blacklisted from Google for spamming, then it'll be hard to get your site to do well in Google because of the penalty applied to that old IP address. Same goes for an IP neighbor who might be penalized for spamming. You'll most likely have to contact the engines directly (not an easy task) and request they review your individual circumstances. This can take *months*.

It's very cheap to add a dedicated IP address to your hosting plan, and this ensures no "neighbor" can land you in hot water. Having a dedicated IP address will not prevent issues caused by a previous domain getting banned for spamming. This rarely happens now, though, as Google is a registrar and can see when IP addresses were issued, to whom they were issued, and so forth. Basically the engines like Google know when the "Bad Guy" gave up that IP address, so they know it's new to you.

Keyword Research: Knowing Where Traffic is

Directing traffic to your blog means you get more visitors to your blog. That mass of Internet traffic is rich pickings for your advertising on your blog. That's where you want to be. The trick to that little problem is hooking into what most people are searching for—by using the most common keywords. So, when users go into their browser, what are the most likely keywords they will type in as a search string? That's the traffic you want to find.

THE IMPORTANCE OF KEYWORD RESEARCH

Okay. Stop what you're doing right now! Stop coding, stop playing with blog pages, stop searching for images, stop writing articles—just stop!

Have you actually done some keyword research for your new blog? Not, "Yeah, I'd search for *xyz* phrase if I were looking for this info." Think of the bigger picture, such as data on who searches for what. Have you sifted through hundreds of phrases related to *every single* page of your blog? Do you know all the phrases users have searched that are related to your content for, say, the past year? Do you know whether they've been searching for the singular or plural versions of phrases?

That is the kind of keyword research we're talking about . . . the nuts and bolts of your topic and its realistic popularity on the Web.

Now that you have a glimpse of the type of data available, we can dive deeper.

WHY KEYWORD RESEARCH IS FIRST

Simply put, you cannot hit the target if you cannot see it. By doing the keyword research first, before you even build a single page, you'll know exactly what content to bring to market from the start. Your ideas of what users *might* like to see will be replaced by realistic knowledge of what they have historically looked for. Doing the keyword research is almost a shortcut to getting started, because the goal is to build a blog that receives good rankings and develops good traffic rapidly.

Your research will help you understand what volumes of searches are performed on the phrases related to your topic. There are two key points to make in this situation:

1. You have to know what keywords people are searching with. *What are people searching for?*

2. You also have to know the volumes of those searches. *How many people are searching for each keyword?*

Building a blog takes time. Getting that blog ranked well takes time. Developing a decent amount of traffic takes time. By knowing exactly what phrases users are using to search with, you can build content to match those searches exactly. By knowing how many searches a phrase generally sees, you can decide whether it's worth your time to build the content that will produce a good ranking for the phrase. Remember, each article or page should be between 200 and 300 words in length, so the time to make a page is a very real commitment, and the investment in the research will pay off.

It's also very important that you get the research right. By using the right tools and knowing how to read the data, you'll know how to find the hidden gems. These hidden gems are the phrases that are *not* overpopulated with optimized pages right now, and yet still get a useful number of searches per day. This concept is known as the "long tail" of search—in effect, you're looking for *niche phrases,* which are narrowly targeted phrases that most folks don't optimize for. Collect enough of these phrases in your list of well-ranked pages, and, collectively, the incremental traffic they deliver can easily outpace more mainstream phrases. We'll get into the "long tail" in more detail in a bit.

First, you need to decide how broad or focused you want to look. If you look at one-word phrases, such as "apple," you'll see a large volume of traffic generated—meaning lots of folks search that phrase daily. This is excellent, provided you can rank well for that phrase. Take a look at who's already on the first page of results for this phrase. Are you likely to knock them out of the first-place spots? Realistically—not immediately.

So, your biggest weapon is to target phrases that are broader in nature, such as "red delicious apple." People searching this phrase actually want information on this exact item. Those searching for "apple" *may* be looking for information on "red delicious apples," but you have no way of knowing this. They may also be researching computers manufactured by Apple Computer Corporation, which is a completely different thing, and quite obviously completely useless to your current purposes.

Take a long look at the areas you're going to cover, and ask yourself whether you can define them even better. If you can, you're on your way to posting a winning blog. The more targeted each page is toward *one* phrase or keyword, the better the chances that the page will be ranked successfully. Sure, there may be only four searches per day on "red delicious apple seeds," but if you rank well for the phrase, you'll likely get traffic from those searches. The result is that by providing exactly what searchers are looking for, the value of your Web site increases in their eyes.

NICHE PHRASES

Now, those niche phrases we mentioned earlier are pure gold. The true "long tail" resides in the phrases you may never have thought of on your own. They are the phrases users cobble together in their own unique way—phrases you may have no idea you rank well for, yet they are phrases that users nonetheless find you listed under.

When starting a new blog, you'll be without some important data that will come only with time. When starting out, simply target the phrases that your research has led you to—those represent the most popularly searched phrases for a given topic. However, when your site is listed in the engines, and you can find yourself in the results, and you are seeing inbound search traffic in your stats, then it's time to get cozy with a great little tool:

www.hittail.com

We've been using this tool since it began running in beta in 2006. It is amazingly useful, though there are likely those who could replicate it and make it better. The point is, it's amazing simply because this type of tool provides you with real-time information that shows you *exactly* which phrases users have used to get to you. It shows you which engines they came from and how deep your Web site is in the rankings there. It will also make suggestions about which phrases you should move to the "To Do" file and begin creating content for.

Users will amaze you with the creative phrases they come up with when searching for things. And these are not phrases you'll ever think of yourself either. These are the crazy, off-the-wall combos that would simply never occur to you when doing the keyword research up front. This data is very powerful because it allows you to create content pages for those niche phrases, phrases you'll most likely rank very well for, and develop a whole new base of incremental traffic. There might only be three to five searches per day on these oddball phrases, but it adds up when you start targeting them.

Another nice benefit is that due to its real-time nature, this provides a snapshot of what users are searching for *today*. Not what they looked at last month or over the past year, but five minutes ago. This allows you to spot trends as they emerge.

RESEARCHING THE BIG PICTURE: TOOLS AND HOW TO USE THEM

To begin your keyword research, you'll need some solid tools to do the work for you. Google doesn't like to share data, so don't look there for any info. Yahoo is happy to share results, as long as all you're after is searches performed on a phrase during the month shown. This is not so good if you are in a seasonal industry, and not so good when a larger time frame provides a truer picture.

If, however, that 30-day snapshot is right up your alley, you can use the Yahoo Keyword Tool for free—inventory.overture.com/d/searchinventory/suggestion. It will show you the results of your search for info with the following restrictions:

- It's limited to only those searches performed through Yahoo.

- It's limited to showing only one month's worth of data. (Note—as of this printing, Yahoo's tool seems to be stuck showing data from several months in the past. This may correct itself, or it may indicate that Yahoo is no longer supporting this tool.)

This means you'll have to do some basic math on your own. If you know the phrase was searched 25,000 times in June, then you could assume that for the year, it's searched roughly 300,000 times. That's fine—as long as the phrase is not seasonal. Following this logic, we could say the phrase is searched an average of 800 times daily.

You'll want to create a spreadsheet to keep track of the data and do the math for you, but in the end you'll have a much clearer picture of what's worth chasing.

What's that? You don't mind spending a few bucks to get a better tool for keyword research? Excellent idea, because, as we all know, you get what you pay for.

Here are two tools well worth mentioning for performing keyword research:

- *Wordtracker*. This tool can be located at www.wordtracker .com. Wordtracker is the more powerful tool and allows you to perform much the same research as the free keyword tool from Yahoo. However, Wordtracker adds the ability to create projects within which to catalog research. This allows you to easily track multiple phrase groups for different sections of your site or different keyword groups for multiple individual Web sites. Wordtracker also allows you to export the data, which is very useful. One downside to Wordtracker is that it's hamstrung by the fact that it uses data from Dogpile and Metacrawler queries over the previous 90 days. These are not hugely busy spaces. So, while more mainstream phrases will show traffic, more niche phrases may not.

Note: Dogpile and Metacrawler are known as "third-tier" search engines. Basically, they are just smaller search engines that many have never heard of in the wake of the bigger brand names. Metacrawler has the added distinction of being an engine that uses other engines to obtain its results. Unlike Google, which has a large cache of the Internet's pages to show in its results, Metacrawler has no such cache and relies on results found via other engines to show you results.

- *Keyword Discovery*. Trellian's Keyword Discovery tool is located on the Internet at the URL www.keyworddiscovery

.com/index.html. In fact, Keyword Discovery is pretty much our first-line go-to research tool for new projects now. It costs some money, but is well worth checking out if you're serious about running your Web site as a business. The Keyword Discovery system looks at roughly the past 12 months' worth of search data from all the major engines. This scope alone affords Keyword Discovery a much better look at what's popular, long-term, with searchers. Keyword Discovery includes lists to save data, the ability to export data, and so on.

The ability to access search query volume data through Trellian's own database or through individual Yahoo data centers makes Keyword Discovery a powerful tool for international users. It also allows enough of a look to understand where seasonal trends lie and will provide estimates of how many times phrases are likely to be searched daily, based on historical data.

Just remember that good tools cost money, but that doesn't mean you must have them. Successful sites have been started using nothing but free tools and standard marketing techniques. You can do the same. As revenue grows, purchase the tools to dig deeper and continue to cultivate further growth.

To give you an idea of how each system varies and the differences in the volumes of search data compared, let's look at this example. For the phrase "jeep," each service returned the following results:

- Free Yahoo tool—558,136 searches in January 2007, so 6,697,632 per year

- Wordtracker tool—4,805 searches in the past 90 days, so 19,220 per year

- Keyword Discovery tool—1,797,149 in the past year

No perfect solution exists but these tools give you a strong place from which to start.

Now You Have Some Data: What Does It Mean?

After using any one of the tools, you'll have a list of phrases with counts next to them. Whether it's monthly or yearly doesn't matter: the simple math mentioned previously will give you a key number—an average of how many times per day a particular phrase was searched for.

Remember, if you're using the Yahoo keyword tool, you'll need to account for the fact that Yahoo has only a percentage of the market share on daily searches. So whatever the number shown by Yahoo, multiply that number by something around 70 percent. Yahoo has 30 percent of the market. We also need to know the other 70 percent of the market to be an effective advertiser. The simple math would be:

Keyword = 34,000 searches per month, according to Yahoo

More realistically, that phrase sees about $34,000 \times 1.7 = 57,800$ searches per month, overall. This is simply a ballpark figure and the actual results will vary. However, this will give you a clearer picture of the reality you're dealing with.

Now you know who's searching what. The next step is to narrow your workload. At this point you may have hundreds of phrases in your spreadsheet. Simply take the top 100 by average number of daily searches and drop them into a new sheet. This will become your working sheet—the one you reference when creating content.

Think of this top 100 list of keywords as your list of 100 pages or articles for which to work on data—or, if the site is already live, the 100 pages to tweak. If you have a live blog and see a phrase that does not match any current content, create a new article or page. Don't try to revise off-topic content to fit a particular keyword—do the work and build the new page to support the keyword.

> Note: Stick to using one keyword (or phrase) per page. This will allow each page to fully support its bid for the one keyword. Want to go after another phrase? Create a new page. Keyword and phrase may be used interchangeably—a keyword phrase is the same thing.

What to Avoid

This one is easy: avoid phrases that are too broad or overly saturated.

Broad phrases are those one-word phrases like "baseball." The results that will appear will very likely be a mixed bag because a word like "baseball" can be used in combination with so many other words, when searching on many hundreds of combos. In addition, being such a highly searched word, a broad phrase like this will be crowded with the heavy hitters of your vertical—like MLB.com (the Major League Baseball Web site). Be realistic. You are not going to beat MLB.com for the phrase "baseball" out of the gate. And probably not even when you are way, way out of the gate.

You are much better served drilling down to focus on more targeted phrases. Things like "baseball batter gloves" or "right-handed baseball batting gloves." This idea goes back to the niche phrases we spoke about. More pages from your site ranking well and drawing smaller numbers, when combined, often outpace the volume of traffic provided by one page found for a busier phrase—and they offer you protection if and when a single page from your site drops in the rankings.

Skip the really busy phrases for now, and skip phrases that are too broad. Overly saturated phrases have so many folks competing to rank well that you're bound to lose out to older, more established sites. If you're not appearing on the first two pages of results (top 20), then the value is greatly diminished for you, so avoid fighting the big guns right away—build strength from the grassroots level up.

In fact, use this thinking to whittle down those phrases from your Top 100 spreadsheet; the revised list of 100 phrases will be the perfect set to get you started—even if the site isn't new.

Have Faith

Finally, when you've done the keyword research, found the top 100 phrases, and weeded out the overly saturated ones and the broader terms, you'll have the list that will help you. Whether you're starting a new Web site or revising an existing one, this is the list of phrases you'll need to start the real grunt work of your blogging project.

Have faith in your list of phrases, and start either building pages to match the keywords or revising current pages to go after selected phrases from the list.

If your blog is brand new, work on getting these 100 pages live and indexed. Fill in the blanks later and in a way that makes sense for the site you're building. Your keyword research list is an item you'll reference time and time again to help keep you on the right path. Update the list every four to six months or so, and you'll have a strong resource for success.

Choosing a Domain

When choosing a domain, there is only one thing you should seriously consider: *Will it be easy to remember?*

If you choose a domain to match a keyword you'd like to be found for in the search engines, you're potentially making things difficult for yourself and your readers. It's tough to find topic-relevant, keyword-rich domains these days. On the contrary, if you get too specific in this search, you could wind up with a domain that's not easy to remember.

Your best bet is simply to think of something unique, catchy, and easy to recall. This will ensure readers can easily pass along the name of your blog to others. This word-of-mouth advertising is a critical part of what makes blogs successful.

By sitting down and brainstorming with a pen and notepad, you'll create a list of phrases or words related to yourself, your blog, or the topic of your blog. Use this list as a starting point to search for your domain.

Blogs are about you and your personality, so don't be afraid to choose a domain that's a bit off the wall. Searching for your own name may be a viable option as well. Always remember that while the topic of the blog might not be about you specifically, your style will come through in everything posted there.

Always keep in mind that if your blog is to be a business and that you might one day like to sell ad space to businesses, it's going to need a professional name. Not anything as dry as MyName Inc.com, but also not as casual as MyDirtySocks.com (taken, by the way), although either of those would probably have a place somewhere.

If you can, keep the name somewhat related to your blog's topic. If not, take a page from one of the most successful brands of all time: Google. Its name is a made-up word and today is known globally, as both a noun and a verb. Look at phrases that describe your blog's topic. Is there an acronym that can be made into a word? The Search Engine Marketing Professionals Organization goes by www.sempo.org. The acronym is much easier to recall, and after a while, SEMPO became another word used in the industry.

As you build your own online business, your domain will become associated with the quality of your work. Good writing, excellent recommendations, good reviews, useful articles, and so on all help build the credibility of a domain. It's important to remember this, as years down the road that domain will have built a value, and it will be too late then to simply decide to drop it and move to another domain you like better.

If you think you have a solid name in mind and want to find out if it's available, the following is a rundown on the process. Where you do this is less important than the fact that you need to do this. Without doing the research to see whether a domain name is available, you're back to square one before you even begin. Getting your blog up and running will require having a domain in hand, so to speak. Follow these steps to check for availability of your chosen domain name:

1. Go to the www.godaddy.com Web site. (Or try www.whois .com, www.register.com, or any of the dozens of domain sellers that can be found through a quick search.)

2. Type your domain name idea into the search box at the top of the screen.

3. Hit the Go button.

There are some options to choose from, too. You might wish to purchase a dot-info, dot-net, or dot-org domain name. Simply select the desired *Top-Level Domain* (TLD) from the drop-down menu, then hit Go. It's best to try for a dot-com name, but others will work if you simply must have that name.

Next, the system will tell you whether it's available. You will quickly know whether your desired domain name is available. If not, it's a long, drawn-out process to try to get it. It might already be in use, or the owner may want a lot of money for it. It's best to simply try for another domain name. Don't ever get too stuck on a single idea.

If the domain you entered is available, buy it quickly. To do this, you'll want to have an account with someone like GoDaddy. Your account could be anywhere, but GoDaddy has some of the lowest prices for buying domain names right now.

The basic process consists of these five steps:

1. Open a free account with GoDaddy (or anyone you choose).

2. Log on to your account.

3. Search for the domain you want.

4. When it comes up as available, there will be a Buy This Domain link shown. Press it.

5. Follow the rest of the checkout procedure.

A word of warning, and GoDaddy is bad for this, as are some other domain name registrars—read everything very carefully, every step of the way. Many times, extra items are included in the purchase as add-ons that you might not want. It's easy to remove them from your shopping cart, but they quickly balloon the purchase price for a domain from under $10 to $30, $40, or more. Also decide on the period of time you want to own the domain. Your basic price gives you one year of ownership, but the checkout system usually sets the default ownership period at two years, thus doubling your fee. You should consider carefully how long you want to own the domain, though. If your domain expires, someone else can buy it and will then own the domain you worked so hard to build traffic on.

In many cases, people choose to buy the domain up front for five or more years to ensure it's in their control for a long time. It's a personal call, but if you're going to pay for only one year, be sure to keep your contact information up-to-date in your account. Your domain provider may try to e-mail you when your domain is expiring, but if it can't reach you, your domain may be sold to someone else, and there's almost nothing you can do about it after the fact.

> Note: Your domain provider may also automatically try to charge you for five years when you renew or buy a domain name. Be careful here, as the costs can increase quickly. In general, though, it's worth considering longer ownership terms with good domains.

WRITING YOUR ARTICLES

Writing a blog is essentially like writing an article for a magazine—just like building a new Web page that you want people to find and to read. Perhaps the single most important thing is the title of your blog.

How to Title a Blog

This is what you are going to call your blog. This title is different from the title you'll use for each article you post. If you're writing a blog on apples, the title of the blog might be *The Apple Blog*. Remember to use your keyword research to target the best keyword or phrase to use in the title of the blog. We define *best* here to mean the phrase you want to be found for with good daily or monthly search volumes.

Writing Article Titles

The key here is to establish the keyword you want the article to rank well for. If you're posting an article on *Red Delicious Apples,* then be sure to include that phrase in the article title. After that, try to write a title that is catchy. Saying *Red Delicious Apples* is fine, but using *The Health Benefits of Red Delicious Apples* is more likely to catch a reader's interest. Just be sure to construct a title that reflects the content the reader will find in the article itself. It's a bit of an art form, but after a few posts you'll get the hang of it.

Using Keywords Properly

As with basic search optimization for a Web page, you'll want to use the keyword or phrase a few times in the text of the article itself. Even if you are simply posting a press release on something related to your topic, you can write a brief introduction to the release yourself, and then perhaps mention the keyword once or twice in the introduction. Press releases are often not written with search optimization in mind, so you will have to take this into account when using them as content for your article. Editing the press release is frowned upon, as the original authors were trying to announce something newsworthy, and changing their copy is not what they expect of folks using the release. For this reason, I usually write a simple introduction or preview myself, with my own thoughts, to ensure the keyword I'm after makes it into the post.

Writing Articles

Writing the articles you will post can seem like a daunting task. Yes, it requires some creativity. Yes, it requires a command of the language in which you're publishing. Yes, you should try to be as professional as possible.

In the end, though, you may simply write down and post your own opinion on a topic. You may choose to follow an event and post press releases to update readers. You may use quotes from other articles and link your readers back to the full article elsewhere. This is the beauty of blogging—you are not constrained by any rules about what is expected, though common sense should lead.

How Much to Write for Each Article

How long should an article be? Blogs are not that different from Web sites, so again, writing between 200 and 300 words of unique, topic-relevant content should be fine for each article you will post. Don't fret if you cannot get past 100 words. Don't fret if you go past 500 words. Use these numbers as guidelines and build from there. You will be surprised how quickly you reach the 200-word mark when you set out to expand on a topic a little bit.

Just make sure to follow the basics about including the keyword phrase a few times in the content and let your fingers do the rest. There are no hard-and-fast rules here, so write as you see fit, following the basic search optimization guideline of mentioning the keyword or phrase you want the article to rank for a few times in the article, ideally near the top. In the big picture, you'll be fine. Some posts will be longer, some shorter. Some will be simple reprints of press releases or a post of a series of images from an event.

Don't try to write a book in every post—your readers will not read it all and the spiders won't care about the extra work.

What to Write About

Well before this point, you will know what the topic of your blog is about. Your keyword research will have led you to discover a host of related items. Begin with that keyword research and start writing. When you begin expanding on the topic itself, start offering opinions on things and updates on the latest news related to your topic; you'll quickly realize there is no shortage of items to base blog articles around. If you haven't figured this out by reading other blogs, they are a great place to express your opinion on things. Good or bad, you'll find some folks who will support you. Even if they don't, the old saying applies: "Any press is good press."

One key point to remember is this: while you're trying to get your articles ranked well in the Search Engine Results Pages (SERPs), always write them for your human readers. Those are the folks who will spread the word about your blog.

As for topics, well, spend some time with your keyword research data. This information will show you exactly what phrases users are searching with, so you'll know what to target for blog articles. Keep an eye on the news sources as well. If there's anything big happening in your world, your blog will have a ready made source of information to write about. Keep it relevant and related to the overall topic of the blog, of course.

Also, keep in mind that long-tail keyword tool we mentioned earlier—HitTail. It's a great source to see what phrases users are using to actually find you. Tracking these alongside the keywords you researched before starting is the perfect way to see your growth on popular phrases (your ranking, basically). If the phrases you found in your keyword research phase start showing up in your HitTail data, it means that users are finding you ranked on those busier phrases—excellent news. Be ready for this to take a while, though. In the meantime, enjoy the gold mine of data this tool provides and use it to help discover new topics to write about.

How to Label Categories

It's a good idea to break your blog up into categories. By doing this you create a clean filing system within which to house your posted articles. It makes it easy for readers to find what you have posted on particular aspects of your topic, and, more important, it allows you to use specific keywords within internal links. These keywords within internal links play a role in how your blog may be ranked by the engines. Skip this option and you're missing a golden opportunity. By the very nature of how blogs are constructed, these internal links with keywords will appear on almost all the pages created when you post articles, so there's no need to go looking for keywords on various pages to link to other areas, as you would on a Web site.

As always, reference your keyword research to determine what you should use when labeling categories. These categories do not need to be labeled with the most popularly searched phrases for your topic, but the keywords used should appear in your research list with some level of traffic on them. There's no point in ranking number one for a phrase with only one search per year on it.

Blogs and Linking

If you already have a Web site up, running, and indexed and are now starting a blog to expand your content offering to users, make sure you link the site and the blog. Using the right anchor text on the Web site can help the blog a bit and, more important, will ensure the blog is found by the spiders quickly. Take the time to look through your stats to figure out which pages are most popular with your users to ensure that, at a minimum, a link to your blog appears on those pages. It's a quick way to get users to find your newest offering and start spreading the word.

Here's what Eric Ward, a link-building strategy expert, has to say on www.ericward.com:

> One of the most crucial linking concepts to understand is that links to web sites serve different purposes for different audiences. Search engines use links to identify patterns or tendencies that can help them identify high quality sites. In simpler terms, the search results or rankings you see at Google, Yahoo, and MSN/Live all are driven in part by the links pointing to those sites. But it isn't as simple as *more links = higher*

rankings. The engines are looking for inbound link patterns that show trust, not manipulation. Content that is unique, useful, and of high quality tends to attract links from other sites that are of a similarly high quality. The science behind link analysis is remarkable and complex, and algorithms can discern through overall linking patterns which sites should be given greater importance, which links matter most, and which sites should rank highest.

If you want to reach out to individual Web sites to request a link from them, here's a great process explained to me by Eric. It's simple and polite. The following is an example of a link request letter.

Hi [Webmaster's name],

My name is [your name] and I work with [Web site's name] to help spread the word about their great [free products/ services/content, etc.]. I was hoping you'd consider mentioning us to your users or linking to us on your [provide the Webmaster with the specific page you'd like to see your link shown on, and include the section, if necessary—be specific]. Please find a brief overview of what we offer visitors below. If you have any questions, feel free to contact me via e-mail or with a quick call. I am a real person and will reply quickly. Thanks again for your time and consideration.

[Your name, Web site URL, e-mail address, and phone number] _____

[Offer a brief rundown about what the site's about and the value it offers.]

Now you'll need to research the site a bit to try to dig up a name to address this to. I suggest using the following steps, as I do:

1. Go to www.GoDaddy.com.

2. Type in the URL for the site you want to request the link from.

3. It'll say the domain is taken but will offer a link to "More information." Click it.

4. Enter the code presented to you and click again.

5. If the owner of the domain name is not paying for private registration of the domain name, you should be able to now see contact information such as a person's name, address, e-mail address, phone number, and so on. The assumption is that the domain owner entered real data. You may not always get a useful result. While domain owners are legally required to enter accurate data when registering a domain, many do not.

Frequency of Posting

This one is simple. Try to post a new article to your blog every day. Failing that, every second day. Bare minimum should be three times per week . . . and not three in one day once a week. You want to keep people interested, not bombarded.

Your goal is to show that the blog is being actively maintained and that fresh content is being added frequently. This will keep the spiders coming back regularly, which will ensure that fresh content is being crawled and indexed by the engines. If you start at the pace of one post a day, after a month or so you'll have shown a solid history. After this, skipping weekends, or even going on vacation for a week, isn't going to pose a problem for you.

You will most likely find that you'll end up addicted to posting things. Soon you'll notice as newsworthy items pass your way, and you'll be posting multiple times each day. This is good for your blog, good for your readers, and good for your business, too.

Moderating Comments

You will have to make a choice on whether you'd like folks to leave comments on your blog or not. All the platforms have the ability to allow or disallow this function. Allowing comments is a great way to build a community with your readers. Also your readers are more likely to spread the word about you when they know you are a real person, and they feel connected to you somehow.

There is a downside, though. Some systems, notably the BBlog platform, end up attracting comment spam. Comment spam is an unfortunate reality of blogging for many folks, though it is manageable. Spammers employ robots that crawl around and look for comment boxes to fill in with their spam message. In systems without captcha codes (those nifty and sometimes overzealously used, pesky little pictures with characters (text and numbers) in them), these robots can post hundreds of comments an hour to one of your posted articles.

If you've set your system to allow comments to go live, they will—leaving the mess for you to clean up and, in some cases, causing the engines to take note of your questionable taste in linking.

Setting your system to moderate comments, though, can limit potential problems for you. You personally will still need to wade through the hundreds of spam comments awaiting approval before being put up on the live blog, but at least they won't go live. Moderating comments is often a good practice in order to keep your good name intact with your readers. This is because most comment spammers are touting adult content and other inappropriate material. Nothing can kill a blog faster than spam comments with hundreds of links to adult content or other useless junk.

A third option should allow you to turn off comments altogether. Each system differs slightly, but it will all become part of a fast process when you learn the system you're on. Do the research first, though, and ask questions about this stuff to make the right choice before you start posting.

I personally have used BBlog. I ran into the comment spam issue and solved it to my satisfaction—meaning it wasn't happening any more. Today I use WordPress exclusively and have fewer problems with spam. An excellent spam blocking plug-in for WordPress is called Akismet (www.akismet.com). By using this one plug-in on your WordPress blog, you can effectively eliminate almost 100% of your spam issues. It captures the spam and holds it for you to deal with, easily letting you bulk delete them all, or target individual comments left by spammers.

One quick tip: if there's an option that allows trackback URLs to be turned off, take it. Turn them off and avoid 99 percent of the spam problems. These URLs are simply the URL for a posted article, shown on the screen. Those robots the spammers use cruise around looking for exactly those URLs to scrape and send their spam to through the comment fields on each post. Turning off this option means they have no URL to scrape.

Note: Robots are programs which scan visible Web pages on the Internet. They search for URLs and email addresses. Don't put email addresses on your blogs and Web sites in the clear, as they will be harvested and added to spam e-mail lists.

SEARCH ENGINE OPTIMIZATION FOR BLOGS

Whether it's a corporate blog, a news-type blog, or even a personal blog, optimizing your blog for the search engines is a must. The blog SEO tips here are courtesy of Bill Hartzer, search engine marketing manager at www.MarketNet.com. Bill also has his own blog at www.billhartzer.com.

You can make some simple changes to WordPress and Moveable Type that will make your blog more search engine–friendly and make the search engines beg for more (more posts and content, that is!).

Optimizing a blog is just like optimizing any other Web site.

The content and pages (posts) must be unique, they must be search engine–friendly, and the site needs links from other Web sites. If it's a new blog, then you first need to make sure the blog software you're using is set up so that it takes advantage of all of the possible optimization features. Then announce it to the world, work on getting some links to it, and start making posts.

WordPress Optimization

If you're using WordPress for your blog software, it's important to make sure that your site is search engine–friendly, meaning that it can easily be spidered by the search engine spiders. Just as with optimizing a Web site, it's important to have good title tags and metatags. Keep in mind that blog software usually uses the title of your post as the title tag, so include keywords in your titles as much as possible.

It's important to set up your blog's software so that the URLs don't contain a lot of variables. Instead, use URLs that include the post title or post name in them. For example, if you're using WordPress you'll need to set the permalinks so that it uses in the URL. You can also set up a specific category for the post archives, and you might consider using a keyword that's related to your blog instead of the default, which is typically the word "archive".

Fintan Darragh of www.dech.co.uk has a great blog post called "Ultimate WordPress SEO Tips" (www.dech.co.uk/2005/11/ultimate-WordPress-seo-tips). Darragh talks about permalink optimization and says, "The goal: stick more keywords up into the URL and remove the faff, which nobody uses, to make the URL search engine and people attractive. Having keywords in your URL is an absolute must, especially when it's as easy as WordPress makes it." He also goes on to talk about getting rid of useless tags like the month, day, and year, as well as one important detail: whatever you do, stick with the site structure you choose—otherwise you might end up with a lot of useless links to your site. Other tips that Darragh mentions are optimizing your page titles and your post titles—and installing a few plug-ins that are useful such as the "Related Posts Plugin" and the "Technorati Tag Generator."

There are several other places where you can get specific tips about setting up WordPress in a search engine–friendly manner, including the following:

- SEO at Aleeya Dot Net (www.aleeya.net/category/Word Press/seo)

- The Best WordPress SEO Possible (www.WordPress.org/ support/topic/49168)

- Search Engine Optimization for WordPress (codex.Word Press.org/Search_Engine_Optimization_for_WordPress)

- Search Engine Optimization for Blogs (www.blog-maniac .com/blog-seo.htm)

- DYI Search Engine Optimization (lorelle.WordPress.com/ 2006/01/15/dyi-search-engine-optimization)

One of the best tutorials out there is one called "DIY Search Engine Optimization" by Lorelle VanFossen (lorelle.WordPress.com). Specifically, VanFossen has some great tips, including how to optimize your code, develop strong intrasite links, write with strong keyword usage, use categories and tags, and use ping services.

> Note: In computer technical terms, a ping is word used to describe a a network test message sent across a network. The Internet is in essence a humungous network. If the web site you are pinging is up and running, you will get a response. In blogging, it's used to alert other sites that you have something new on your own site.

VanFossen says that "the goal is to help search engine crawlers move through your Web site collecting information to be stored in the search engine's database." The following five tips are key to successfully getting your blog's data into a search engine's database:

1. Make sure there are no road blocks in the path of a search engine crawler.

2. Make sure the crawler can move through your blog, examining all your Web pages.

3. Provide adequate keywords and key phrases that clearly help categorize your content.

4. Provide clearly labeled tags and categories recognized by tagging service crawlers and many search engines today.

5. Take advantage of pinging services.

Several WordPress plug-ins are available that will help you take advantage of internal linking (like the Related Posts Plugin), which will link to other posts in your blog that are on the same topic. Other plug-ins that might be helpful are plug-ins that automatically generate a Google Sitemap file, as well as plug-ins that help you categorize the site, such as the WordPress Subdomain Plugin (www.webguerrilla.com/WordPress-subdomain-plugin).

Diane Vigil, an acknowledged expert in the field of blogging, has the following advice for WordPress users—it's a great hit list to work through in order to make your blog a bit more "Web site–like" in how it appears to the search engines. We're bringing you the complete post from Vigil's blog, with permission. Pay attention folks. This next bit is worth its weight in gold:

Make your WordPress Blog a Real Website: Must-Have WordPress Edits and Plugins

While WordPress is great blogging software, I find that it (like many blogs out there) lacks some basic features that could make it more usable—that is, what I call a real website. That people can use. Of course, all this is strictly In My Opinion. But hey.

Gotta have menus on all pages: Uh . . . I don't even know what to say about this. The WordPress folks, in their wisdom, have seen fit to remove menu links (or the "navbar", if you will) from permalink pages (that's single.php). I fix that right away. Web pages are supposed to have menu links to other pages of the site. End of story.

Turn Category and archive pages into tables of contents: By default, WordPress displays entire posts on what it calls the "archive" pages (category and monthly pages, etc.). That eventually means that those pages will be too long—so, on those pages, WP limits the number of posts to the number you've chosen to display on your home page (who knew that little secret?) and surrounds them with annoying previous/next links to yet more archive pages with a limited number of posts and previous/next links—follow them and you eventually wonder where you are.

This "feature" also means that posts are displayed in full on their respective permalink pages, Category pages, Monthly, Daily and Yearly pages, and maybe on the home page too. Geez, Louise and hello duplicate content! A post should only be displayed on the home page (temporarily) and the permalink page (single.php). And archive pages should simply display a list of titles (with, perhaps, excerpts of the posts). Period.

(1) To turn full-post archives into post title listings: the code for archive.php (which controls all this):

```
<?php while (have_posts()) : the_post(); ?>
```

```
<li id="post-<?php the_ID(); ?>"><a href="<?php the_perma-
link()?>"rel="bookmark" title="Permanent Link to<?php
```

the_title(); ?>"><?php the_title(); ?></a><small>-<?php the_time('m/d/Y') ?></small></i>

<?php endwhile; ?>

If you're hyper about blurbs, stick this in there as well:

Replace this:
<?php the_content() ?>
with this:
<?php the_excerpt(); ?>

(2) Site Map: Aha. One of the more annoying aspects of most blog software is the inability to get an overview of just what is on the site. At one glance. Not only do I not want to travel around in circles trying to find out what the author has written, but I don't want to poke around from one category to the next. Let's see a site map, yes? For WordPress 2.0.x (and up, I think), we have Aleister's DagonDesigns SiteMap Generator (http://www.dagondesign.com/articles/sitemap-generator-plugin-for-wordpress). I wrote about how to implement it here: (http://developedtraffic.com/2006/09/12/sitemap-for-wordpress-2x) and am using it here: http://developedtraffic.com/sitemap.php.

=> I am terribly sad that Narchives: http://weblogtools collection.com/archives/2004/05/23/sortable-nicer-archives-for-wordpress has not yet (to my knowledge) been updated to work with WP2.0.x. Narchives was short for "Nicer Sortable Archives"—a sitemap that allows users to display listings by date, category or title. Very handy. Even for me on my own blogs. <grin> Someone attempted to update it, but I couldn't get it to work properly. I wish for this . . .

Recent Posts: As a companion to the site map, the WordPress wiki's Recent Posts hack at http://wiki.wordpress.org/Recent%20Posts allows you to display a list of your most recent posts on your home page. Far better than an "Earlier

Posts" link on the home page . . . taking you to a page with a limited number of posts and Earlier/Later links and . . . (anyone see a pattern here?). Just plunk the code into your my-hacks.php page and upload it, enable legacy my-hacks.php file support (in Options > Reading), slip a little code into your template, and it'll display links to your most recent posts. It's configurable: if you're displaying five posts on your home page, you can set it to display links to post #6 on, up to the number you specify. Mine's at the bottom of the home page here: http://developedtraffic.com.

Recent Comments: Arrive at your favorite blog wondering if there are ongoing discussions about earlier posts? Brian's Latest Comments plugin at http://meidell.dk/archives/2004/09/12/brians-latest-comments from Brian Meidell offers just that functionality. Download it, upload and enable it, create a new page where you'll add a little of Brian's code, and there you are. A link to mine is here: http://developedtraffic.com/recent-comments.php.

Removing Nofollow: No fan of nofollow, for the first time in WP2.0.x, I was unable to remove it—but found Dean Edwards' Nofollow Remover Plugin: http://dean.edwards.name/weblog/2005/03/nofollow quite excellent. Throw the code into your my-hacks.php file, upload it to your WordPress root, enable legacy my-hacks.php file support (Options > Miscellaneous), and you're done.

Scripty-Goddess' Comment Subscription Manager: This is a good one—someone comments on your blog but has no way of knowing whether more comments were posted afterwards. I don't think people generally spend their time re-visiting posts (or loads of older posts, no matter how interesting) to find out if anyone's replied since their last visit. This is where the illustrious ScriptyGoddess steps in with her WP Subscribe To Comments plugin: http://www.scriptygoddess.com/ archives/2004/06/03/wp-subscribe-to-comments, which allows commenters to opt to receive email notifications of later comments. Just download it, upload to Plugins and activate, add a little code below your comment box, and there you go.

But wait! There's more! WP Subscribe to Comments also has a comment subscription manager; just create a new page, plunk the code into it, and people can manage their own subscriptions (so you won't have to). Terribly elegant. Here's mine: http://developedtraffic.com/wp-subscription-manager .php.

ADDED: Mark Jacquith has taken over development of the Subscribe to Comments plugin: http://txfx.net/code/ wordpress/subscribe-to-comments, which now has even more features (such as the ability to subscribe to a post without commenting). Most excellent; I'll be upgrading.

WP Untexturize: I guess I can be fussy about code; at any rate, Scott Reilly to the rescue with WP Untexturize: http://www .coffee2code.com/archives/2004/06/27/plugin-wpuntexturize which I thought I'd throw in here.

Basically, wptexturize() (located on your server in the folder/ file: /wp-includes/functions-formatting.php), performs certain character and text replacements that I'm not too groovy with, namely this (') being replaced with (‘) or (&#8217), and (") being replaced with (“) or (”). I appreciate the other character and text replacements that were happening, just not those.

Alternate Font Sizes: I haven't tried this one yet, but just read fernando_graphicos' (he of the wonderful graphic design talent and ever-dwindling font sizes) Easy Javascript Text Resizing: http://fernando-graphicos.com/easy-javascript-text-resizing. Nice. Easy to understand.

Akismet: If you haven't tried Akismet: www.akismet.com, then you're probably not blogging with the kind of unpestered-by-spammers calm that you could be.

Well, that's it. I hope this is of help to you all—and, if you've got (or know of) some great plugins, please mention them here!"

Diane can be reached via either of her blogs at www.dianev.com and www.developedtraffic.com.

Movable Type Optimization

If you're using Movable Type for your blog software, then it's also important to make sure that your site is search engine–friendly and can be spidered by the search engine spiders. As with optimizing a Web site, it's important to have good title tags and metatags. Keep in mind that blog software usually uses the title of your post as the title tag, so include keywords in your titles as much as possible.

Miles Evans (www.webpronews.com/expertarticles/expert articles/wpn-62-20060310MovableTypeSEO.html) says that "Movable Type is optimized quite well out of the box, but there are a few quick tricks to easily providing the spiders with some dynamic content." He goes on to say that you need to optimize your template. "For my main home page and category index pages I hard-code most of my metadata. Your metatags will be at the top of the template within the head tag. You can get fancy on your index pages but I cannot really see why. Optimize these two templates by hand for whatever keywords you are targeting site wide."

Evans has another article titled, "Best Movable Type Plugins" at: www.webpronews.com/expertarticles/expertarticles/wpn-62-20060310BestMovable TypePlugins.html, which talks about his favorite plug-ins that help him get great search engine rankings. His favorite Movable Type plug-ins for SEO are Dashify, MTPaginate, MT Blogroll, MT InlineEditor, MT-Textile, BigPAPI, as well as Ajaxify (a set of plug-ins that adds several ajax/javascript widgets into the Movable Type interface), CheckLinks, FormatList v1.0, and Better File Uploader for uploading files.

Nicholas Carvan (his site is down at the time of printing) had a great article about Movable Type optimization called "Optimizing Your Movable Type Blog for Google." In it he talked about PageRank (and how it relates to your internal linking on your blog), having keywords in your URL (which is important for all blog optimization), and blogrolling. He defined the term blogrolling very well, saying, "Blogrolling: Inbound links are gold, but in Google's eyes, not all links are equal. In particular, Google isn't wild about links contained within JavaScript—apparently they can index them, but that doesn't mean they always want to."

Once you've set up and configured your blog's software, it's important to make sure that you leave it alone—if you change your page URLs, then any links that you've received from other bloggers may not be valid anymore. If you need to change your site's structure (perhaps you've been blogging already and wish to use the tips from this article to optimize your blog), then you might want to take a look at the Objection Redirection WordPress Plugin (Word Press-plugins.biggnuts.com/objection-redirection-WordPress-plugin) if you're using WordPress. The Objection Redirection Plugin gives you a simple interface to redirect users (and search engine bots) to the proper page, especially if you've changed your site's structure.

START BLOGGING

The best thing you can do is to start blogging. Go ahead and post to your heart's content and write, write, write about your topic. The more content you can provide, the better. If you're looking for a general rule of thumb when it comes to the amount of content needed on each post, we suggest that you include at least two to three paragraphs of information. Depending on your site's overall Web design, your post's pages (pages other than the home page of your blog) might look light on content if you have only one or two paragraphs of text. In one particular blog I write daily, I chose a Web design (i.e., WordPress theme) that forces me to write at least three paragraphs of text. If I write any less than that, it just doesn't look right: there's a large amount of blank white space right there in the middle of the page. In some cases, it's helpful to use examples, screen captures, company logos, photos, or other images to fill some of the space in posts if you believe that you're going to end up being light on content.

Feel free to link out to other blog posts that are related to the topic you're writing about. For example, before you publish a post, go on over to your favorite blog search engine and find another recent post on the same subject—and link to the post. Linking to other bloggers will get their attention, and hopefully they'll end up linking to you as well. If other bloggers have trackbacks turned on, then their blog will link back to your post. Some trackbacks are moderated, so it might take some time before your link shows up on the other blog. And some bloggers have trackbacks turned off, so a link back to your site might take some manual intervention.

Categorize your posts as much as possible and whenever appropriate, and feel free to add categories as you blog—it will help the internal linking structure of your site and help the search engines and users find on-topic posts. Keep in mind, though, that if your blog has an overall theme or topic, it's helpful to try to predefine a dozen or so categories and stick to them. Too many categories can end up leading to a mess, and if your categories are listed in the sidebar, they could end up making you write longer and longer posts, just to keep up: your sidebars could be rather lengthy, thus requiring you to write more content in each post to fill up the white space that will be left over on the page. Generally speaking, it's helpful from a search engine–optimization standpoint to have at least two or more posts in each category; and putting posts in more than one category could lead to duplicate content issues down the road.

Blog Content

You can include many different types of content in your blog posts. Certainly, the type of blog will dictate some of the content—but there always comes a time when a blogger suffers some sort of writer's block. Additionally, how often you update your blog depends on the type of blog and the subject—some corporate blogs might be updated as infrequently as once a week. Some blogs that tend to follow the news can be updated as often as several times a day or several times an hour. Generally speaking, though, if the content is funny, topical, controversial, or newsworthy, then it will get links from other Web sites and from other bloggers. In the blogging world, links from other bloggers and other Web sites are key to a blog's success in the search engines.

The following is a list of the types of content that could be included on blogs:

- A blog can always talk about or mention something in the news. If it's mentioned in the news and it's related to the blog's overall topic, then it could be blogged about.

- A good way to get links from other bloggers is to write about what other bloggers are writing about. Want a link from another popular blog? Consider reading that blog and expanding on one of its recent posts—and be sure to mention the other blog site and link to it in the post.

- A good way to receive some traffic from the search engines and from the blog search engines is to blog about something that's very popular or something that's in the news or that's headline news everywhere. Even if that headline news or breaking news isn't related to your blog's topic, you can always find some reason to blog about it. Consider, for example, a top news story that plagued the headlines for several weeks: Someone carrying a contagious disease flew around the world knowing that he was carrying the disease, and it was a top story for a while because of the public health concerns. My marketing blog covered the story— and explained how a person's name was a top search term on the Internet for a while. It just so happened that the search results for this man's name (the top search term) weren't very flattering, and there would continue to be an online reputation management issue in the future for him.

- Tutorials, whether big or small, can lead to great content on a blog. Consider a post on an automotive blog that tells you how to buy a used car—this type of content could be popular among the site's visitors and could lead to links from other Web sites and other automotive bloggers.

- Blog posts that include a specific number of steps or reasons can be popular. Consider, for example, that a post on a weight loss blog titled "10 Ways to Lose 15 Pounds before Summer" might be a timely blog post in the spring.

Duplicate Content Issues

Duplicate content issues tend to be the most troublesome issue plaguing bloggers—duplicate content on blogs, in my opinion, is typically the biggest reason why blogs don't rank well in the search engines. And it's not an issue related to an individual blog or how someone designs it (the blog's Web design) or which theme or template is used—the whole premise behind blogs is generally the problem.

Blogs were originally designed to be someone's "personal journal," so to speak: they were meant to be updated on a regular basis, providing a means for others to keep up with what the blogger is doing. Blogs were designed to include ways to navigate around the blogger's posts—by viewing posts by category (which is a good idea) and by navigating through the use of calendar-type internal links (which is bad). The search engines generally like it (and reward us) when a blog or other type of site links to content that's related to other content on the site. So, linking posts or pages by categorizing them is helpful to the search engines and helpful to the site's visitors: we tend to like to view Web pages that are on a certain subject or that are categorized properly. (However, when was the last time you went to a blog and decided, "Gee, I wonder what this blogger was thinking on January 17 last year?") Or, have you ever thought, "I would like to see a list of all of the posts that this blogger made last February." These are two reasons why blog posts shouldn't be linked via a calendar-type system—no one uses it. However, the most important reason calendars shouldn't be used on blogs is because it leads to duplicate content—which ends up causing all sorts of search engine ranking issues. Furthermore, if there are too many internal links on a Web site, the links tend to be discounted, and some overall link credit that has been garnered (Google calls it PageRank) is spread too thin around the site. By limiting a blog's internal linking to only categories and other occasional links among posts, the "link credit" is passed to only the important pages on the site: the home page of the site of the categories and the individual posts.

It's been known for a while now that search engines do not like to index and keep track of the same content over and over again: it fills up their disk space, slows down processing, and generally contributes to a bad user experience when we look at search results (who wants to read the same information over and over again, anyway?). By limiting a blog's internal content to the home page, the categories, and the individual blogs, you're staying away from these potential duplicate content issues. Additional internal links that should be removed are the PREVIOUS and NEXT links. Typically, these links appear at the bottom of the main page of the blog and ultimately create additional duplicate content. Ideally, a blog will be free of duplicate content if the blog has only two ways that visitors and search engine spiders can get to the individual posts from the home page (in the form of a link to the last several posts) and through the site's categories.

Plug-ins

Many good blog software packages, including WordPress, have what are called *plug-ins*. These are small programs or scripts written by third-party vendors or individuals that provide additional functionality to the original out-of-the-box installation of the blog software. There are many useful plug-ins, depending on what you want to do with your blog. Too many plug-ins, though, can end up ruining a blog's ability to rank well in the search engines, so I would be careful when it comes to plug-ins, choosing only those that are really needed. Some of the plug-ins will have no effect on the site's optimization, and some will have a big effect.

The following types of plug-ins are helpful:

- Plug-ins that generally deal with blog spam or comment spam are helpful. Some plug-ins will check to see whether the person making a comment on your blog is a human (this is helpful). Some plug-ins that verify trackbacks (automated links from other blogs) are helpful.

- Plug-ins that automatically translate a blog's content into other languages can be helpful. These types of translator plug-ins could allow a site to be indexed in many different languages, opening up the potential readership base. Translating a Web site into another language does not equate to duplicate content—although the content is in English and in French, the content is unique and not considered duplicate.

- Plug-ins that automatically create metatags such as a meta description tag can be helpful.

- Plug-ins that help the blogger create Technorati tags can be helpful. Technorati is a search engine on the Internet, specializing in searching blogs.

- Plug-ins that fix other miscellaneous duplicate content issues can be helpful. For example, plug-ins are available that will make sure that only the www.domain.com version of a blog is available; otherwise, when humans or search engine bots request a page on domain.com, they're automatically redirected using a 301 Permanent Redirect to the equivalent page on www.domain.com. Having two versions of a site (one on domain.com and one on www.domain.com) can lead to duplicate content issues.

The following types of plug-ins are generally not helpful and will lead to optimization issues and hurt a blog's ability to rank well in the search engines:

- Plug-ins that create extra internal links to other Web pages or other posts on the site in an automated fashion can contribute to duplicate content issues.

- Plug-ins that ultimately lead to the automatic creation of additional pages on the blog can be optimization killers. These types of plug-ins can include the automatic creation of archives, calendars, additional navigation, or randomness (e.g., links to random posts).

- Plug-ins that automatically create additional pages on the site based on any type of searching by visitors could lead to additional duplicate content issues.

Here is a list of the current plug-ins that Duane uses on some of his blogs right now:

- Akismet (www.akismet.com) effectively deals with most spam, enabling you to concentrate on writing posts rather than on managing spam.

- Dofollow (www.semiologic.com/software/wp-fixes/do follow). Since most WordPress applications are set up with the default settings, spiders are told to *not follow* any links you post up. Users can click them easily enough and go to the site as expected, but the spiders are basically told to ignore the links. I use this plug-in to ensure that any link I place on the site is capable of passing some value to the site I'm linking to—and to make sure the spiders can get there from my link.

- SEO Title Tag (www.netconcepts.com/seo-title-tag-plugin). This thing flat-out rocks! It'll take a quick edit to the */header.php* file in your */wp-content/themes/name-of-your-selected-theme* folder, but it's an excellent tool and works as advertised. I love using this plug-in in conjunction with a keyword research tool to check for the latest keywords worth chasing down. A couple hours of your time and a good keyword research tool, and you're on your way to much better traffic.

- Sphere Related Content (www.sphere.com/tools#wpwidget). This neat little item imports a small list of related-topic news stories for your readers. It places an unobtrusive link just below your content or post, and when a reader clicks it, it opens a window over the page displaying related information on the topic.

- Text Link Ads (www.text-link-ads.com). These guys offer a free plug-in when you create a free account. You install it like any other, and when it's active, you can control which text link ads appear on your site. While the entire process is a bit more complicated than that (Duane gets into it elsewhere in the book), it's easily managed, and I can honestly say that these guys pay bloggers on time. Caution should be exercised when selling links on your site—Google takes a dim view of this and sometimes penalizes sites which do this.

- Trackback Spam Control ( ). The folks over at Rice University created this little number—and it's still quite effective, so I continue to use it.

Promoting Your Blog

Whenever you make a post in your blog, your blog software will attempt to ping certain sites to let them know that you just updated your blog. There are many blog ping services out there, including Ping-O-Matic and Pingoat. Your blog software can be configured to ping sites automatically, and ping lists (lists of URLs to ping) are readily available from many bloggers who have blogged about them. A good ping list will contain at least 50 or more Web sites that are notified each and every time a post is made on the blog. You can easily find up-to-date ping lists by searching for them (keyword "ping list") at your favorite search engine.

If your blog is new or you would like to get some additional links, you can submit your blog to blog directories as well as to other sites that will list your blog (don't forget to submit to DMOZ.org, Yahoo! Directory, and the Best of the Web Blog Directory). About.com has a great article about promoting a blog (weblogs.about.com/cs/blogpromotions/a/promoteblog.htm), and even Biz Stone has a great tutorial about promoting your blog (help.blogger.com/bin/answer.py?answer=1060). Finally, don't forget to turn on your blog's RSS feed. And if you're looking to promote your RSS feed, try searching your favorite search engine for "promote rss" to find a lot of good tutorials.

Links from other blogs are very important to a blog's search engine rankings. A good way to boost up a blog's search engine rankings and popularity is to get links from other blogs that share the blog's same topic. Other bloggers are always flattered when someone comments on something that they write on their blog. So it's very helpful to participate on a regular basis by commenting on others' blogs. This will boost the blog's possibility of getting a permanent link from the other blog as well as, in many cases, the possibility of getting visitors and the search engine robots to see links back to the blog.

Many sites compile lists of the world's most popular blogs. By participating in (commenting on) and linking to (mentioning) those bloggers' posts in your blog posts, you increase the chance of getting links from some of those popular blogs. Some popular blogs have a lot of visitors every day. Your comments on their blog could bring visitors to your blog and help with the blog's overall link popularity.

Other ways of getting additional links include paid or sponsored links or paid or sponsored reviews. There are services that allow you to pay for reviews (of your blog) and receive payment for reviewing other blogs. It's important to be aware, though, that paid or sponsored links may be scrutinized by the search engines in the future, so buying links or reviews or receiving money from sponsors for links may be an issue and could have a negative effect on a blog's ability to rank well in the search engines.

Using social bookmarking and social networking communities can be very helpful when promoting a blog. Generally, the idea is that the more people you can tell about your blog content, the more chances you have to get links to the blog or blog post—which will ultimately help the blog's ability to rank well in the search engines. Many bloggers tend to congregate or hang out in certain places and on certain social bookmarking and social networking communities. Sites like MyBlogLog, Del.icio.us, and Digg can help bring attention to blog posts. Keys to success include adding friends and networking on those sites.

Promoting your blog is just like promoting a Web site—you need good spiderable content, links to your content, and you need to set up your blog software to take advantage of all the great features.

Where to Submit Your Blog/RSS Feed

Allowing the spiders to crawl your blog and index it is great, but with blogs, you can be more proactive. There exist a number of directories and Really Simple Syndication (RSS) or feed aggregators, which accept blogs as well as feed-type submissions.

Since your blog platform will allow you to syndicate your published content (meaning it's easily packaged for sharing with others), it's a simple process to send your feed URL to these places for inclusion and distribution.

Each service has a slightly different sign-up process, so read the terms and conditions carefully and follow the rules. Some require you place a small bit of code into your blog somewhere, and you should do this. Without this exchange, the service may not accept your feed for distribution. Unlike Web sites, this reciprocal exchange is the way to go right now.

Here's a list of some of the popular places to submit your blog or feed:

- www.getBlogs.com
- www.feedburner.com/fb/a/home
- www.Blogtopsites.com
- www.globeofBlogs.com
- www.technorati.com
- dir.Blogflux.com
- www.newsgator.com/Home.aspx
- www.Bloglines.com
- www.feedster.com/add.php
- www.topix.net
- www.Blogwise.com
- www.boingboing.net

There are many, many more places to submit your blog and feed to, other than those listed here. This list should get you started. It's not necessary to be listed in them all.

For those using blog platforms that allow you to ping them when you make a new post, this list is useful. Most blog services allow you to ping them each time a new post is made on your blog.

This helps keep them up-to-date on when you publish fresh content. Blog platforms automate this process for you, and this list will help ensure every post you make is spread far and wide.

If you are using WordPress to power your blog, place this list in the following space:

Admin>>Options>>Writing>>Update Services

Simply enter the list into the window provided—one entry per line—and each post you make will reach out to all the services to update them. Other platforms will offer the same facility, but its placement will vary from platform to platform. This is the list:

- www.bblog.com/ping.php

- www.1470.net/api/ping

- api.feedster.com/ping

- api.feedster.com/ping.php

- api.moreover.com/ping

- api.moreover.com/RPC2

- api.my.yahoo.com/RPC2

- api.my.yahoo.com/rss/ping

- www.bblog.com/ping.php

- www.bitacoras.net/ping

- blog.goo.ne.jp/XMLRPC

- www.blogdb.jp/xmlrpc

- www.blogmatcher.com/u.php

- blogsearch.google.com/ping/RPC2

- www.bulkfeeds.net/rpc

- www.coreblog.org/ping

- www.mod-pubsub.org/kn_apps/blogchatt
- ping.amagle.com
- ping.bitacoras.com
- ping.blo.gs
- ping.blogg.de
- ping.bloggers.jp/rpc
- ping.blogmura.jp/rpc
- ping.cocolog-nifty.com/xmlrpc
- ping.exblog.jp/xmlrpc
- ping.feedburner.com
- ping.myblog.jp
- ping.rootblog.com/rpc.php
- ping.syndic8.com/xmlrpc.php
- ping.weblogalot.com/rpc.php
- ping.weblogs.se
- pinger.blogflux.com/rpc
- www.pingqueue.com/rpc
- rcs.datashed.net/RPC2
- rpc.blogbuzzmachine.com/RPC2
- rpc.blogrolling.com/pinger
- rpc.britblog.com
- rpc.icerocket.com:10080
- rpc.newsgator.com

- rpc.pingomatic.com

- rpc.tailrank.com/feedburner/RPC2

- rpc.technorati.com/rpc/ping

- rpc.weblogs.com/RPC2

- rpc.wpkeys.com

- services.newsgator.com/ngws/xmlrpcping.aspx

- signup.alerts.msn.com/alerts-PREP/submitPingExtended .doz

- www.topicexchange.com/RPC2

- trackback.bakeinu.jp/bakeping.php

- www.a2b.cc/setloc/bp.a2b

- www.bitacoles.net/ping.php

- www.blogdigger.com/RPC2

- www.blogoole.com/ping/

- www.blogoon.net/ping/

- www.blogpeople.net/servlet/weblogUpdates

- www.blogroots.com/tb_populi.blog?id=1

- www.blogshares.com/rpc.php

- www.blogsnow.com/ping

- www.blogstreet.com/xrbin/xmlrpc.cgi

- www.holycowdude.com/rpc/ping/

- www.imblogs.net/ping/

- www.lasermemory.com/lsrpc/

- www.mod-pubsub.org/kn_apps/blogchatter/ping.php

- www.newsisfree.com/RPCCloud

- www.newsisfree.com/xmlrpctest.php

- www.popdex.com/addsite.php

- www.snipsnap.org/RPC2

- www.weblogues.com/RPC/

- xmlrpc.blogg.de

- xping.pubsub.com/ping

- xping.pubsub.com/ping/

*Please note: The list above was accurate when this book was written. Due to the speed and frequency at which things change on the Internet, some may not work now. Having them in your ping list will not hurt anything, however.

How to Place Ads

Let's start with the great graphic from Google shown in Figure 2.9.

The graphic shown in Figure 2.9 can be viewed online at the following URL:

www.google.com/images/adsense/en_us/support/
blogtimize_en.jpg

Google has vast amounts of data on which positions for ads perform best. There's no sense in us guessing to determine where to start. It's all laid out in the diagrams.

Figure 2.9 focuses on where to place Google ads, but any program's ads will work. You should fully read the program's guidelines and rules. They will spell out how many ads you can show on a given page. Google's system will automatically turn off extra ads.

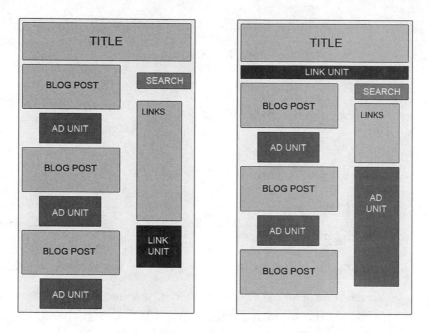

FIGURE 2.9: WHERE TO PLACE ADS IN A BLOG.
From https://www.google.com/adsense/support/bin/
answer.py?answer=43869, reproduced with the express permission of Google Inc.

Some programs will allow you to place an unlimited number of ads on a page; others will not, by design. You will need to experiment and test to determine the right mix for your blog within a program's limits.

If your ad program has limits like Google's (which says you can only show three ad units, one link unit, and one search box per page), you may need to limit the number of posts shown on your main page or place the ad code directly into your HTML code exactly where you want individual ads to show.

The key to physically placing ads is to remember to place ads in spaces that put them in direct view of readers. Since readers are interested in your posts or articles, having ads at the bottom of every post is a really good way to ensure they are seen. In general, larger ads will outperform smaller ads and text links will outperform graphic-based ads. Since these are generalizations, the watch-word is still test, and just try it out for yourself.

Blogs are made up of very few elements. You have what is essentially an index page, which you can think of as your main/home page, and you have a "post" page.

The index page of your blog will have a running list of the most recent posts you've made. Depending on how you have your blog programmed, the actual number of posts being shown on the index page will vary. Careful testing will show you whether you should allow your system to show the full post on the index page or only show a snippet and encourage readers to click a "Read More" link to view the complete post.

The trade-offs are as follows:

- By showing the entire post on the index page, you allow readers to see the article easily, increasing the ease of use of your blog. This does not encourage page views, as users have no reason to go anywhere other than your index page. Getting users to read other, older posts is left up to your "Archives" link.

- By placing only a snippet of text from each post on the index page, you save space and encourage users to click to read each full post. This will increase your page views and potentially drive revenue from ads higher. (Showing a user more ads often results in higher clicks.) It does require readers to click more to read things, which can erode readership.

- In short, it's a balance between page views for you and ease of use for readers. Testing both options on your index page will quickly show you what works with your readership.

- If you're using a text underlining ad system like Clicksor provides, then actual ads are placed according to the keywords you enter into its system. Tell the system to turn "sports" into an ad, and then that word will be linked by the Clicksor system in your posts.

Be aware of limitations:

- There are limits to how many ads you should place on your blog. Respecting the reason your readers come to you is critical. They are not there to view 10 to 15 ads on your blog. They're there to read what you've written today. Many bloggers approach advertising in a unique way—they simply post up and tell readers this is how they pay the bills.

- Your readers know why you have ads in place; so by posting up each day about advertisers, you offer them exposure and communicate with your readers a critical message— you're here to blog, not to tout.

- If your goal is to make a living from your blog, then you are seeking to find more readers rather than place more ads on your blog at once. Fewer ads in front of a blog reader will result in less advertising revenue; more ads can erode readership and put people off.

- One idea to keep in mind is to place advertising text links in your sidebar or link lists. You can place links from affiliate programs in this list as you would any other link. Typically, readers will look through your link list to see what other areas of your blog or Web site might interest them. This is a great place to showcase advertising text links that can generate revenue for you.

SUMMARY

Blogging is meant to simplify online publishing. Although you may feel, after reading this chapter, that there are a vast number of choices to be made and it's tough to know where to begin. The fact is, it really is a simple process:

- *Resources.* Look at your budget, both time and money. Choose a system that fits both.

- *Keyword research.* You won't know where you're going if you don't have a map. Keyword research is your map.

- *Consistency.* Get a schedule laid out and stick to it. If you can write only twice a week, that's fine, but be sure to do it.

- *Relevancy.* Don't go off at a tangent. Try to stay focused on your topic. It might feel great to rant about your commute that morning, but if the blog is about anything other than rants or commuting, it's off topic, so save it for somewhere else.

- *Getting a blog started!* The single most important point, though, is that you do something. Make a decision—any decision. You can upgrade later if you need to, you can cancel an account later if you need to, and you can even do more keyword research later, if needed. The single biggest barrier to most people succeeding is that they never get started in the first place.

If you choose Blogger to start with, then a year later want to move on to WordPress, don't sweat this now—just get started. If you've got some experience already, then this decision may be a simple one. Those of you who are new to the game may agonize over the future and where you'd like to be.

Just remember, *if you don't start, you'll never get there.*

Make the decision now, get started today, and, as you learn and grow, tomorrow will sort itself out. And if it doesn't sort itself out you can help, because you'll know more tomorrow than you did today.

GENERATING REVENUE **WITH YOUR** BLOG

WHAT'S IN THIS CHAPTER?

How long will it take you to make money with your content and your blog?

Building a blog with great content and getting it to rank well is a great thing. If you've done the building and optimizing correctly, you'll see traffic start to increase and page views start to climb.

There's no way to make easy money. You have to be patient, positive, and persistent.

As a reality check, let's discuss timelines at this point. The goal here is to make money with your blog. Fair enough. But the basics of business still apply. It's improbable that you'll place your blog live online and within weeks begin seeing revenue. Sure, you might see a dollar or two every few days, but what we're after is more like hundreds or thousands of dollars per month—something real, something you can actually use.

A lot of talk exists about whether Google has a "sandbox"— a place where new sites go to "age" before being included in the general search results. Google denies it exists, and while we're not going to say it *does* exist, we will say that about a year after one of our sites went live, there was suddenly a large increase in inbound search-related traffic from, guess who? . . . Google.

The idea of "aging" a Web site certainly makes sense. It gives the site a chance to establish itself, grow its content, and get the bugs sorted out. It also allows Google to watch things for an extended period of time to judge whether the site is real or just some fly-by-night site that won't ever get updated or expanded.

Google likes sites that receive frequent updates, so using this time (it varies, but let's say one year, because that ballpark figure is realistic) to add more content and fine-tune internal cross-linking is a very wise move.

Having a blog that makes money takes work and an investment of time. Be prepared to run through several months of you updating content and not generating much revenue.

After you emerge from the sandbox or aging period or whatever you want to call it, you will see traffic begin to increase and, along with it, revenue. More traffic equals more revenue—it's a simple equation. This doesn't mean you won't see traffic from other efforts such as link building and some basic directory submissions. It simply means it'll take a while for sites like Google, Yahoo, and MSN/Live to become larger drivers of traffic to you.

WHICH AD PROGRAMS TO CONSIDER

When considering different types of ad programs to use, three main types of ad programs come to mind. They are contextual ads, ad networks, and affiliate programs.

Contextual Ads

What is a contextual ad? Contextual ad systems put advertisements on your Web site that are in the same context as (closely related to) the content of the Web page where you place those advertisements. The easiest way to explain context is to demonstrate by example. Figure 3.1 shows two blogs owned and

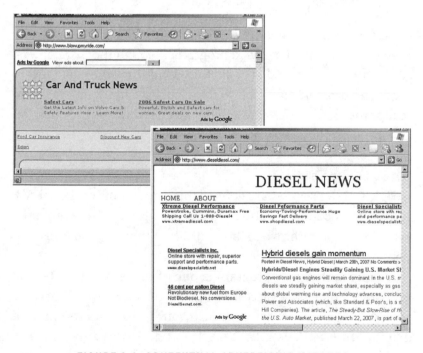

FIGURE 3.1: CONTEXTUAL ADVERTISING MATCHES
THE CONTENT OF A WEB PAGE.

managed by one of the authors of this book. One blog is about cars in general, and it has Google contextual ads about cars. The second blog, shown in Figure 3.1, is about diesel engines in automobiles, and thus its contextual advertising is all about diesel fuel.

While this section primarily covers suggestions based on the Google AdSense platform, the recommendations will work for any contextually based ad system and placement suggestions, and it will also work well for image-based ads.

Here's a short list of contextual ad programs you should consider:

- Google AdSense (https://www.google.com/adsense/login/en_US)

- Yahoo Publisher Network (YPN) (publisher.yahoo.com)

- Clicksor (www.clicksor.com)

As with many things online, those are not the only sources. We have used these contextual ad programs, though there are others. At the time of writing this book, these options represent a few of the bigger programs available, but they all have limits and rules. So read through the rules carefully, or just send in your application and if you don't qualify you will be rejected.

GOOGLE ADSENSE

Google's AdSense program defined this category of contextual ads. It's the granddaddy. It's also stable, performs well with even modest amounts of traffic when thoughtfully optimized, and, most important, Google pays on time.

Google's AdSense program is one of the original contextual programs bloggers can access. It offers a reliable way to show contextual ads to your readers and turn your traffic into revenue. In general, Internet ads follow the Internet Advertising Bureau's standard ad sizes and formats. Some of the specific options and settings for Google AdSense advertisements are as shown in Figure 3.2.

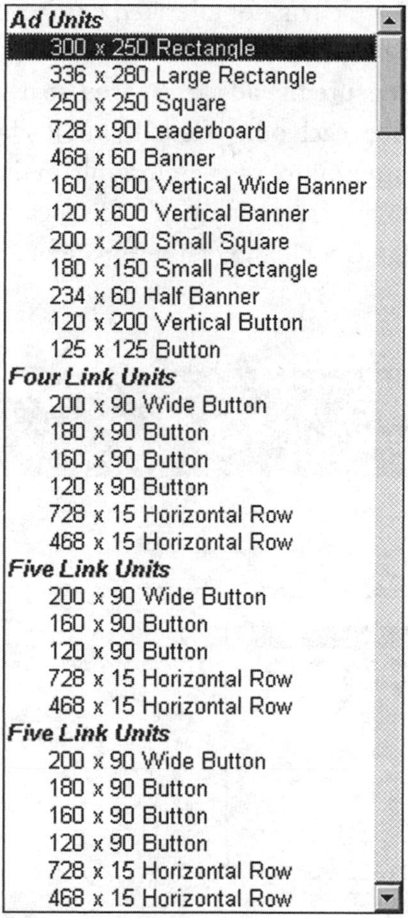

```
Ad Units                                    ▲
   300 x 250 Rectangle
   336 x 280 Large Rectangle
   250 x 250 Square
   728 x 90 Leaderboard
   468 x 60 Banner
   160 x 600 Vertical Wide Banner
   120 x 600 Vertical Banner
   200 x 200 Small Square
   180 x 150 Small Rectangle
   234 x 60 Half Banner
   120 x 200 Vertical Button
   125 x 125 Button
Four Link Units
   200 x 90 Wide Button
   180 x 90 Button
   160 x 90 Button
   120 x 90 Button
   728 x 15 Horizontal Row
   468 x 15 Horizontal Row
Five Link Units
   200 x 90 Wide Button
   160 x 90 Button
   120 x 90 Button
   728 x 15 Horizontal Row
   468 x 15 Horizontal Row
Five Link Units
   200 x 90 Wide Button
   180 x 90 Button
   160 x 90 Button
   120 x 90 Button
   728 x 15 Horizontal Row
   468 x 15 Horizontal Row          ▼
```

FIGURE 3.2: GOOGLE ADSENSE ADVERTISING FORMATS.

To set things up, follow these simple steps:

1. Open an account on https://www.google.com/adsense/
   g-app-single-1.

2. Follow the wizard to build your ads.

3. Copy and paste the supplied code into the chosen space on
   your blog.

4. Minutes later, ads related to your content will begin to appear.

In the past Google has not tolerated competing ad providers. However, Google has recently revised its rules. It's still plainly your responsibility to ensure the ads are spaced apart from each other and do not resemble each other visually, but it's fair game to place ad units, even from multiple ad vendors, all on the same page.

Figure 3.3 shows a screenshot of adding Google AdSense advertisements into a Google Blogger template.

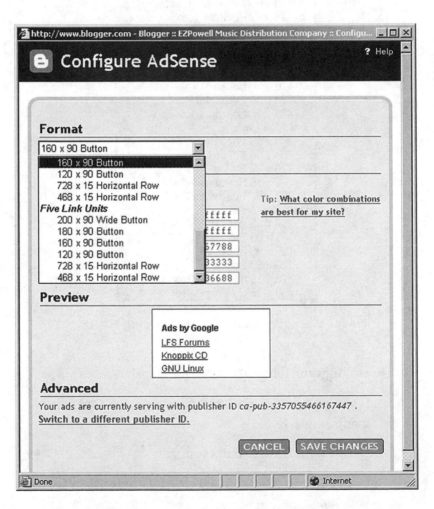

FIGURE 3.3: ADDING GOOGLE ADSENSE ADS IN A
GOOGLE BLOGGER TEMPLATE.

FIGURE 3.4: GOOGLE ADSENSE EARNINGS REPORT EXAMPLE.

Figure 3.4 shows the Google AdSense earnings report for a new blog one of the authors has just created. At the time of writing this book, the click-through ratio (CTR) is a little low. That is because this blog is very new. Figure 3.5 shows what's possible with an optimized blog, decent traffic, and well-placed ad units.

> Note: CTR is a number of clicks divided by the number of impressions. The number of impressions is how many times an ad has been displayed on your page.

YAHOO PUBLISHER NETWORK (YPN)

Yahoo's program is still relatively new, but reports suggest it at least holds its own against Google's AdSense and, in some cases, even outperforms Google's offering. This is where your testing pays off down the road—to determine which works best for you.

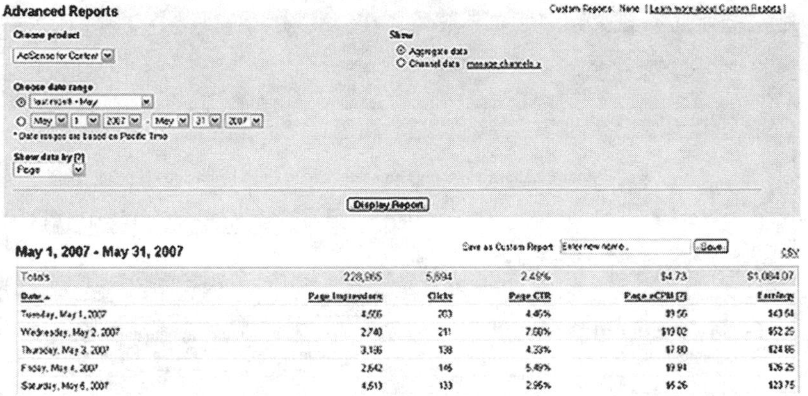

FIGURE 3.5: GOOGLE ADSENSE OPTIMIZATION

INCREASES TRAFFIC.

Yahoo Publisher Network is similar to Google's AdSense program. When you place the Yahoo ad code in your blog's HTML code, ads matched directly to your blog's content are shown on your live pages. It's a proven combination that results in solid click-through rates (CTR) and steady revenues for publishers.

By matching ads directly to the content of the page, the ads shown relate directly to what the users are most interested in at the very moment they load up the Web page.

CLICKSOR

Clicksor can offer bloggers a great way to monetize their content while keeping their blogs clean and visually ad-free. Some bloggers find themselves in a situation where they have used all the available space on their blogs and have no way to easily fit conventionally sized ads into the mix.

Clicksor offers publishers an option to select particular words within the text of the page that appear underlined, similar to a text link. An example Web page with Clicksor links is shown in Figure 3.6. When a user hovers over the linked text, a small box is displayed with the advertiser's message. If the user clicks on the linked text or the display box, the publisher (i.e., you, the blogger) is paid. An example of this is shown in Figure 3.7.

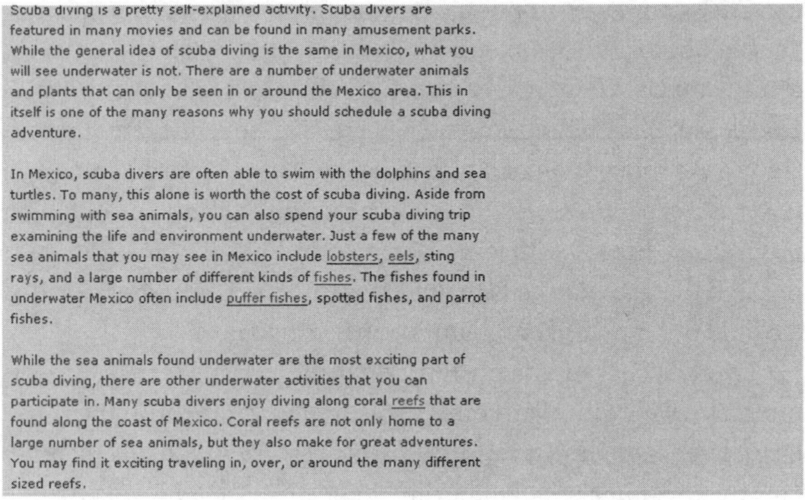

Scuba diving is a pretty self-explained activity. Scuba divers are featured in many movies and can be found in many amusement parks. While the general idea of scuba diving is the same in Mexico, what you will see underwater is not. There are a number of underwater animals and plants that can only be seen in or around the Mexico area. This in itself is one of the many reasons why you should schedule a scuba diving adventure.
In Mexico, scuba divers are often able to swim with the dolphins and sea turtles. To many, this alone is worth the cost of scuba diving. Aside from swimming with sea animals, you can also spend your scuba diving trip examining the life and environment underwater. Just a few of the many sea animals that you may see in Mexico include lobsters, eels, sting rays, and a large number of different kinds of fishes. The fishes found in underwater Mexico often include puffer fishes, spotted fishes, and parrot fishes.
While the sea animals found underwater are the most exciting part of scuba diving, there are other underwater activities that you can participate in. Many scuba divers enjoy diving along coral reefs that are found along the coast of Mexico. Coral reefs are not only home to a large number of sea animals, but they also make for great adventures. You may find it exciting traveling in, over, or around the many different sized reefs.

FIGURE 3.6: CLICKSOR MINIMIZES THE ADVERTISING FOOTPRINT WITH LINKS.

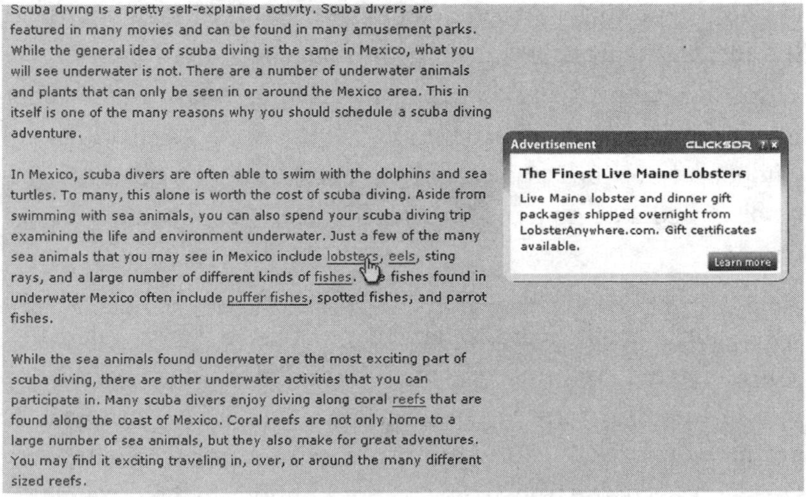

Scuba diving is a pretty self-explained activity. Scuba divers are featured in many movies and can be found in many amusement parks. While the general idea of scuba diving is the same in Mexico, what you will see underwater is not. There are a number of underwater animals and plants that can only be seen in or around the Mexico area. This in itself is one of the many reasons why you should schedule a scuba diving adventure.
In Mexico, scuba divers are often able to swim with the dolphins and sea turtles. To many, this alone is worth the cost of scuba diving. Aside from swimming with sea animals, you can also spend your scuba diving trip examining the life and environment underwater. Just a few of the many sea animals that you may see in Mexico include lobsters, eels, sting rays, and a large number of different kinds of fishes. fishes found in underwater Mexico often include puffer fishes, spotted fishes, and parrot fishes.
While the sea animals found underwater are the most exciting part of scuba diving, there are other underwater activities that you can participate in. Many scuba divers enjoy diving along coral reefs that are found along the coast of Mexico. Coral reefs are not only home to a large number of sea animals, but they also make for great adventures. You may find it exciting traveling in, over, or around the many different sized reefs.
Advertisement
CLICKSOR
The Finest Live Maine Lobsters
Live Maine lobster and dinner gift packages shipped overnight from LobsterAnywhere.com. Gift certificates available.
Learn more

FIGURE 3.7: CLICKSOR USES POP-UPS WHEN A LINK IS DETECTED.

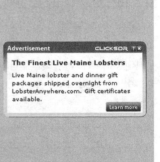

Clicksor is a good option when you place a priority on space or choose not to show conventional ads. As already stated, until recently, you could not use other ad programs on the same page as Google AdSense advertisements. Using Clicksor concurrently with Google AdSense is a good way to make it look like your blog has fewer advertisements—and also to perhaps augment your blog posting text directly with less obtrusive text link ads. However, bear in mind that too many ads make a Web page look like one big ad— it would put me off. How about you? Don't do it.

Overall, Clicksor is a great product and has some great uses. It integrates well with Web content and allows you to limit the number of larger ads shown to users. The ad count will actually increase on your site, but a small underline beneath selected words (words that you choose yourself) is much less obtrusive than graphic banners and such. In fact, graphics provide the lowest revenue return of all types of ads—textual ads make the best revenue.

Ad Networks

Next we have ad networks. An ad network is a broker or reseller of advertising space; it could be a group of advertisers or a group of publishers. In your case, as a blogger, you are the publisher of the ads, publishing the ads on your blog. An ad network acts like a broker by aggregating collective advertising requirements from many sources and advertising on many Web sites, blogs included. Ad networks are capable of performing targeted and intensive media campaigns for specific products, building brand names.

Ad networks run the gamut from small niche entities, such as www.sportsdirectinc.com, to large companies like www.valueclick .com, offering up hundreds of millions of ad impressions per month to advertisers. Signing up for a network is simple, but again, many have rules and minimum requirements. While there are plenty to choose from, some recent additions to the mix include networks specifically targeting those who run blogs.

Note: A brand name is advertising lingo for a household name of a given product, such as Google, Yahoo, or Jeep. One of the authors of this book has a brand name, or at least a stage name, for a band called EZPowell (pronounced "EZeePowell"). And that's me (Gavin), trying to build a brand name for my band, in this book, using this book as a publisher for my advertisement.

Again, here's a short list of ad networks you should consider:

- Blogads (www.Blogads.com)

- CrispAds (www.crispads.com)

- Blogsvertise (www.blogsvertise.com)

BLOGADS

Blogads is a recent addition to ad networks. You sign up, if the company think they have advertisers that might like to be seen on your blog, and you meet its requirements, you're in. These guys do all the advertiser relationship work. All you have to do is approve ads from advertisers who want to be seen on your blog. If you don't like a particular product that wants to advertise with you, it's your call. The goal of Blogads is to bring both sides together—advertisers and publishers, while making it easy for publishers to get what they want with a minimum of interaction. Figure 3.8 shows the log-in screen for the Blogads Web site.

As a publisher, you sign up, list the space you have available and your prices, and wait to hear from advertisers who want the space.

It does take some doing to join the network. Blogads runs a first-class network, so it insists on vetting blogs before inclusion. The same vetting goes for advertisers as well, so bloggers can be assured that only quality advertisers, who also pay for their advertising, are involved.

Bloggers can access individual ads to place on their blog. If your blog's topic matches an advertiser's goals, bloggers may even

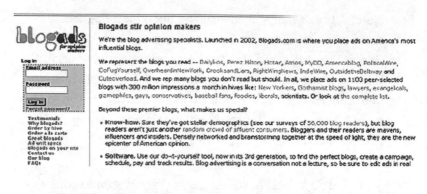

FIGURE 3.8: BLOGADS ADVERTISING PROGRAM HELPS YOU MONETIZE YOUR SITE.

find themselves being somewhat sponsored by an individual advertiser.

Typically, bloggers should expect to earn modest amounts of revenue each month. Blogads states, "The average blogger makes $50 a month selling Blogads, with some pulling more than $5000 monthly."

You are in complete control of the advertisers who advertise on your blog. In fact, you get to write your own ads to attract advertisers to your blog. By allowing bloggers to write clear ads inviting advertisers to check out their blogs, both parties can avoid any back-and-forth, and concentrate on finding opportunities that match their goals.

As already implied, sign-up is not straightforward. Either a current member of the network must introduce you, or you can e-mail Blogads and ask to be matched with someone. It's a unique system that ensures the quality of the blogs being included in the network.

CRISPADS

CrispAds is another blog-centric ad network. It is another company offering a product specifically focused on bloggers. You select the types of advertisers that best match your needs. You name your prices each month, and CrispAds does the work of tracking down potential advertisers to buy your space. One standout feature is the ability for smaller, lower-traffic-volume sites to piggyback on an ad buy with others. This gets the ads up on your site while ensuring the advertiser has the overall exposure it wants. Figure 3.9 shows a screen for CrispAds.

The CrispAds system allows you to show graphic ads or text-based ads. Payouts are solid, and the minimum payout level is a very low $5.00. No need to wait until you accumulate the bucks—these guys start sending you cash fast.

They believe that you, the blogger, are capable of making decisions better than a computer. To this end, you can search for advertisers by keyword rather than having contextual-based ads shown. If your blog touches on various topics, this is a good option that can help keep the ads focused.

Like most ad serving systems, CrispAds offers you a full range of stats to help you understand what's working and when to make changes.

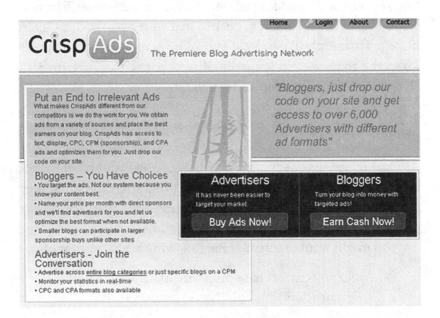

FIGURE 3.9: CRISPADS IS BLOGGING FOCUSED ADVERTISING FOR PUBLISHERS.

One limitation of CrispAds is that in order to receive payments, a blogger must have a PayPal account. CrispAds does not currently offer direct deposit to your bank account, nor will the company send you a check.

Sign-up is simple. Fill in the eight or so blanks and go check your e-mail account. CrispAds will review your blog and let you know if you're approved for the network.

Blogsvertise

Blogsvertise, located at www.blogsvertise.com, is another revenue-generation opportunity for bloggers. Basically, when you are accepted into the program, you are given an advertiser to speak about. You don't need to really review that advertiser per se, but rather, Blogsvertise wants you to work in three or so links to the advertiser in an article. When you've met the required, outlined goals, you submit the article's URL for approval. There is a waiting period during which you must leave the post live, and upon completion of that period, you're paid for your support of the advertiser. The network does periodic checks to ensure that your past articles stay in place permanently. Basically, if you remove the links or the posts down the road, you no longer qualify to participate. Figure 3.10 shows one of the Blogsvertise screens.

Affiliate Programs

Affiliate programs are another way to monetize your blog. Essentially, they are the same as any other ad program, except that they are solely focused on one product or service—and they usually pay a heck of a lot more than contextual programs.

You might want to consider the following affiliate programs:

- Amazon.com (affiliate-program.amazon.com/gp/associates/join)

- Commission Junction (www.cj.com)

FIGURE 3.10: BLOGSVERTISE IS ANOTHER GOOD SOURCE OF ADVERTISING REVENUE.

The trick is getting affiliates to pay. The two just mentioned are completely reliable as far as being paying affiliates (this does not mean the dozens of other programs are less reliable, but do your research first). It is, however, a challenge to get users involved with them and thus generating revenue. While contextual programs pay by the click, affiliate programs tend to pay by the sign-up, or as a result of some other action, such as an outright purchase.

While it may take many more users clicking a given ad or link to make money with an affiliate program, getting the combination right can make steady revenues for you each month. Rather than pennies per click, you'll be paid a percentage of a set value, usually of the sale. In some cases, you'll get a flat-rate fee as well—it depends on the program and what the advertiser has set up.

Note: One really important point when using affiliate programs is this: they thrive on volume. So, if you don't have
the volume, perhaps one of the other options is best
for you.

While you can do well with just the right offer in front of just
the right users, typically, they require a combination of large volumes of traffic, savvy ad placement, and knowledge of what your
users actually want. One real drawback is that the advertisers themselves may not have the ad size you want. If this is the case, it's not
really an option to contact them and request the size you want.
They might do this for a top-performing Web site, but not for a new
addition to their program.

Still, users flock to affiliate programs, and it's easy to see why.
Some programs pay out hundreds of dollars weekly (on average) to
each affiliate. We'd all like to believe that by placing their ads on our
blog we'll suddenly be seeing hundreds of dollars each week or day.
And with some programs it's completely plausible, given the
proper circumstances.

Sell a few items a week for an advertiser whose average sale is
$600 and who shares 10 percent or more of that with you, and you'll
quickly see a couple hundred dollars in revenue each week. Increase traffic, sell more, and the sky is the limit. Most programs
even pay you more when you start selling larger volumes.

The trouble is getting users of your blog engaged in such a way
that they meet the requirements of the program so you earn
money. Read the program requirements carefully before signing
up, or it will become a waste of your ad impressions and space.

AMAZON.COM

Amazon is an example of a company running its own affiliate program that invites Webmasters to join and generate income. Amazon operates one of the oldest affiliate programs online. Today's
program is a far cry from the original days when the only offering

was books. Amazon's program today offers Webmasters the opportunity to integrate ads offering books, electronics, magazine subscriptions, auto parts, and more.

Chances are good that Amazon has something to offer everyone.

Figure 3.11 shows one of the Web sites run by Gavin. This particular page is seriously oversaturated with ads. There are Google AdSense ads at the top of the page, then pictures of all my books underneath (circled in the big ellipse in Figure 3.11). The pictures of the books are invisibly linked to the Amazon listing for each book, and I get a small commission on any sales as a result of the link from my Web site.

One of the keys with the Amazon program is to make sure you place relevant ads in the correct spots. Got a section of the blog talking about adventure travel? Place ads for adventure travel books

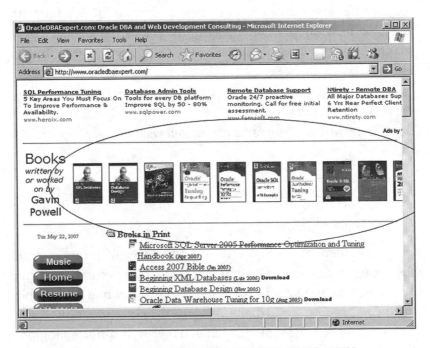

FIGURE 3.11: AMAZON.COM AFFILIATE IMAGE LINKS.

only in this space—and use picture ads, too. Other programs may have items that cost much more than a book, so watch carefully to see what the product is and how it relates to your site. Even though Figure 3.11 shows relevant image links to Amazon, there are few problems with these links. First, they are images, and when people click on them and go directly to one of my Amazon listings, they will either buy or be annoyed. Second, the images are not clear enough.

COMMISSION JUNCTION

Commission Junction is one of the oldest affiliate program sites on the Net and offers a clearinghouse-style system. They exist to bring many programs together for you under one domain. You sign up with Commission Junction, then select the programs you wish to be involved with. Each program will individually approve or deny you , but once approved, you're free to go take some ads for the offer you think will work best and place the ads on your site. Commission Junction tracks all the stats and makes the payments directly to you. Like Amazon, Commission Junction is reliable.

OTHER AFFILIATE PROGRAMS

Some other affiliate programs are as follows:

- www.linkshare.com

- www.bidvertiser.com

- affiliates.ebay.com

While there an almost unlimited number of programs out there, please choose carefully. It takes a lot of investment in time and money to build a solid affiliate program, and many reputable businesses choose to run their programs through outlets like Commission Junction and LinkShare. If you review an affiliate program that sounds too good to be true, then it probably is.

OTHER SOURCES OF REVENUE

Of course, there are ways to make money with your blog other than just publishing other people's blogs on your own blogs and Web pages. Two other types of revenue, or *spin-off revenue*, are *referral revenue* (referring to other things or people, because lots of people look at your blog), and *personal revenue*, whereby you make money doing things like presentations and consulting (because your blog parades your wonderful, expert-level skills).

Referral Revenue

Referrals can be another source of revenue. Basically, you receive a payment for each user you refer to the advertiser. Payments and programs vary, so read the fine print. Watch for the duration of a cookie's lifespan. A *cookie* is an item placed on a user's computer that tells the tracking system when that person first started into the cycle. If the cookie is set to expire at the end of 30 days, and the user does not complete the desired action within that period, that user is of no value to you.

> Note: Many affiliate programs are of this type—set to expire in a short period. They are looking for you to refer a client to them who takes action quickly.

Selling Your Services

If your blog is a self-promotional-style blog, it's entirely possible to develop business from it. If you have a skill or offer a service, your blog may be the best space to showcase this and attract new clients. Developing personal revenue in this manner is completely plausible. A blog of this focus would typically have fewer ads on it as well. The focus is to sell your services, not to generate clicks on ads.

If your blog falls into this category, it's essential you make it as easy as possible for users to contact you. Be sure your contact information is clearly shown, at the top of the main page, if possible.

> Note: Placing an e-mail address clearly visible on a Web site will subject you to spam. There are programs on the Internet, called bots, that look for e-mail addresses. Bots were discussed in a previous chapter. If you don't want to display an e-mail address, use an e-mail form, whereby the user fills out a form and clicks a button to send you an e-mail message. Your e-mail address is still in your Web page, but it's not blatantly visible. The general rule of thumb is this: do not put an e-mail online anywhere, unless you are prepared to start receiving spam. One very old trick is to type out the entire address like this: duane at theonlinemarketingguy dot com. Since the robots look for the @ symbol and the dot (i.e., the period) to indicate an e-mail address, this fools some (but not all) of them.

SELLING PRODUCTS FROM YOUR BLOG

Your blog may be designed to sell products. This requires that you have a solid knowledge of online sales cycles, and you will need a stable *cart* system to handle the ordering, payment, and fulfillment end of things for users who purchase from you. This leads us into a completely different topic best left to the myriad products and resources designed to help e-commerce users. We can say that it takes a lot of time and effort to get set up properly, and some money, too, as good e-commerce systems do not come cheap.

If you wish to sell products directly, then PayPal can be used as a payment processor, and many Webmasters and bloggers simply track transactions via e-mail. It's doable, but selling online requires an investment in credibility. And there is always eBay.

MORE WAYS TO MAKE MONEY

You may have a simple wish to be paid for your opinion. Many wish they could make money for offering their thoughts on a product or service. Well, now's your chance. ReviewMe, found at www.reviewme.com, is shown in Figure 3.12. ReviewMe pays you to review things. As with all programs, read the fine print to make sure you qualify.

ReviewMe handles linking you with an advertiser seeking a review. You provide the review, in your own words, but you follow a prescribed template suggested by ReviewMe. You are paid upon verification that your review has been published on your blog. There is a delay built into the system to ensure your review remains live for a period of time, but you shouldn't be trying to game the system anyway.

Bloggers typically review items or services related to their blog's topic, and there are limits on how many items you can review at any one time. The goal in the end is to have you write unique content about a product or service and drop a link to that product or service into the text you write. You are selling a link, basically.

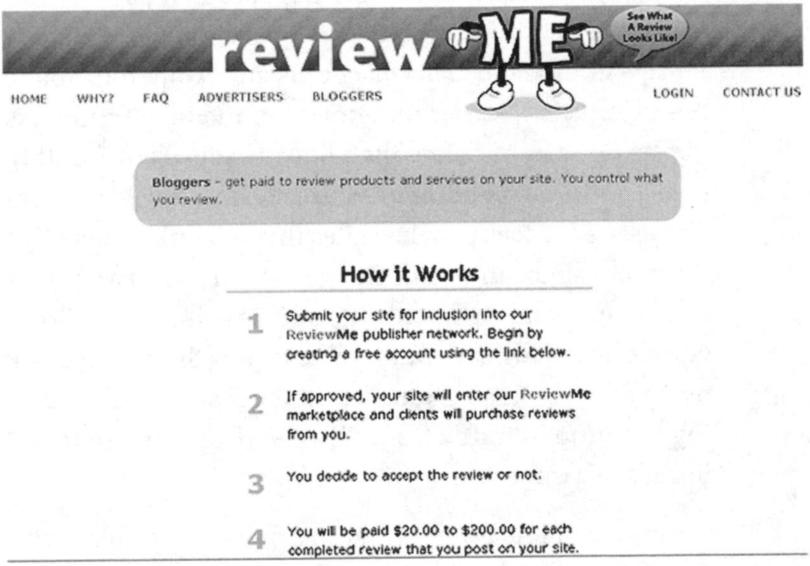
review ME
See What A Review Looks Like!
HOME
WHY?
FAQ
ADVERTISERS
BLOGGERS
LOGIN
CONTACT US
Bloggers - get paid to review products and services on your site. You control what you review.
How it Works
1 Submit your site for inclusion into our ReviewMe publisher network. Begin by creating a free account using the link below.
2 If approved, your site will enter our ReviewMe marketplace and clients will purchase reviews from you.
3 You decide to accept the review or not.
4 You will be paid $20.00 to $200.00 for each completed review that you post on your site.

FIGURE 3.12: REVIEWME PAYS YOU TO REVIEW OTHER PEOPLE'S BLOGS, PRODUCTS, AND SERVICES.

ReviewMe says that "You will be paid $20.00 to $200.00 for each completed review that you post on your site." That could add up in a hurry. But remember, you should state that you are getting paid for the review.

Since we're on the topic of selling links, there is a great resource available to help you with this process. Text Link Ads (www .text-link-ads.com) exists to match you up with advertisers who wish to purchase links from well-run blogs. There are a couple of things to keep in mind when doing this:

1. Your blog will generate more money if it's already established and has decent traffic and PageRank values from Google. (PageRank values work on a scale of 0 to 10, with higher being better in Google's view.).

   Google isn't particularly fond of blogs selling links. Its PR system is based on the idea that if you link to others, it is because they are worth linking to in some regard, not because they're paying for the link. Since a small bit of the PR value of your page floats over to support their page, it's basically like selling a commodity. Google watches for these for-sale links and usually discounts any value from you to the advertiser. It's your call, however, and long-term links in place tend to fair better than links swapped out monthly. (Note: As of the publication of this book, Google has officially stated it does penalize sites that sell links—not all of them, not all the time, but Google watches for it and takes various measures it deems fitting. These may range from Google not allowing any link value to pass through the link on up to its repressing your site in the search results, leading to a drop in traffic from Google. If you choose to sell links, do so carefully.)

Text Link Ads (TLA) gives you some free tools to play with as well. The first one is the Text Link Ads Calculator, as shown in Figure 3.13. This handy tool helps you see the value of any links you might wish to place on your blog. It allows you to test place-

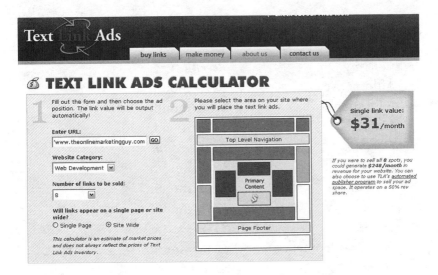

FIGURE 3.13: TEXT LINK ADS CALCULATOR.

ment and category in order to determine which is the most profitable combination for your blog.

You enter your blog's URL, select the category, select the number of links you're willing to sell (more links do not always means more profits), and select the placement where the links would appear on your blog. TLA calculates the potential revenue for you if all your spaces were to sell each month. The results rest on the advertisers who get to review your site to determine whether they'll actually buy links from you. TLA will send you a monthly payment for any sold links.

It's best to keep the links you're selling related to your topic. For example, an automotive blog would choose to sell links from the Automotive category, not the Web Development category. To give you an idea of the range in revenue across different categories, based on Figure 3.6, with the only changes to select a different category each time, we'll run through the entire category list as it stands right now. The examples are based on the sample blog seen in the Enter URL section of Figure 3.13, the individual categories selling eight links each, and assuming sitewide links. Here are the

potential revenues for each category if we'd managed to sell all
eight links:

Category	Revenue*
Automotive	$296/month
Education	$296/month
Finance	$376/month
Gambling	*$496/month*
Politics	$248/month
Real Estate	$312/month
Technology	$248/month
Travel	$312/month
Web Development	$248/month
Other	*$224/month*

These figures are estimates, and your results may vary.

You can see there is a pretty big difference between the lower
end of this scale and the upper end. We cannot stress enough, however, that you only show ads related to your topic. If you were showing Web Development links on a cooking blog, it's unlikely your
users would ever click the links. Lack of clicks means unhappy advertisers who don't return, so the revenue dries up. In addition, in
some cases, it may not be legal for you to link to certain Web sites.
Online gambling is illegal in the United States at the time of this
printing, so be careful about taking links from gambling sites, as
it's also prohibited to support gambling sites. In fact, a number of
Web sites have been contacted by the Department of Justice during
the past year because the sites were deriving revenue from
gambling-related activities. Linking to gambling sites and being
paid for it is deriving revenue from gambling-related activities.

While it's unlikely the DoJ will come looking to speak to you
about a couple of links on your blog, your users might take a dim
view of it if it's not the main topic of the blog, so plan carefully
when choosing which category of links to showcase on your blog.

Yet another source of revenue for you may be to sell white papers or e-books from your blog. Thousands of white papers and
e-books are available online for free, many of which encourage you

to share them with your users. Some may stipulate the item must be passed on at no charge, however, and such rules should be respected.

In fact, a better use of white papers or e-books would be to house a collection of them on the blog, offer them free to readers, and use them to help grow your readership. More readers means more page views, and by using the free offerings to drive traffic, other sources such as Google AdSense or the Yahoo Publishers Network may become a source of greater profits because of the higher readership numbers on your blog.

Personal Revenue

What is meant by *personal revenue?* In the context of this book, it's all about making money from your blog, either directly or indirectly. The advertising on your blog pages, when ads are served to blog readers, is your driving force for reading a book called *How to Make Money with Your Blog* in the first place. However, being the entrepreneur that you are, you are going to want to keep expanding on new ideas for potential revenue. Some successful business people might say that the keys to making money in any venture are continually expanding into new ventures, letting go of ideas that do not turn a profit, and creating spin-offs from successes you already have. In other words, keep coming up with new ideas. Keep those that work. Discard those that don't. An ideal state of affairs might be to create multiple profit centers that all help to feed off of, market, and promote each other. That's an ideal situation, of course. Nothing is perfect, but we would all like it to be sometimes.

So, how does all this apply to *How to Make Money with Your Blog?* For example, one of the authors of this book runs a number of blogs. Here are Duane's blogs:

- Jeep, Land Rover and Range Rover News (www.ajeepthing .com/jeep-blog)

- Car and Truck News (www.blowupmyride.com)

- Diesel News (www.dieseldiesel.com)

- Online Marketing Help (www.theonlinemarketingguy
  .com)

The preceding blogs return advertising revenue on a monthly basis. In addition to the advertising revenue, the author also consults and helps other people as a paid consulting expert in various fields. That's a spin-off from his blogs. People understand from Duane's blogs that he really knows what he's doing. As a result, other bloggers are more than willing to compensate him financially to help them do things like set up their own blogs in the hope that those blogs generate advertising revenue. Duane is also an Internet marketing expert and an advertising professional, and he is frequently engaged to give presentations and talks at conferences and the like. The author is an expert in his field. That is, of course, why Duane gets to write this book.

Essentially, Duane can give expert advice for a fee and perform tasks for others as a revenue stream, in addition to his blog advertising revenue. His blogs have become a showcase for his knowledge and his past work and contributions. Duane uses his blogs and Web site (www.theonlinemarketingguy.com) as a way to advertise himself and sell his skills. He is also known online as SportsGuy.

The coauthor of this book offers number of services, many of which are linked to the Internet. These are Gavin's Web sites and blogs:

- Internet Marketing for Musicians (ezpowellmusic.blogspot
  .com)

- Gavin's Day Job Web Site (www.oracledbaexpert.com, a site
  that includes books and the author's past life as an Oracle
  DBA)

- The EZPowell Band Web Site (www.ezpowell.com)

- A Promotional Presence on MySpace (www.myspace.com/
  ezpowell)

There are probably 50 other Web sites with music and video uploads, including YouTube (www.youtube.com/ezpowell)

- Major Internet retailers. Gavin's books and music CD releases can also be purchased on Web sites such as amazon.com, barnesandnoble.com, cdbaby.com, itunes .com. For these search items search for gavin powell or ezpowell.

So, what's the point of the preceding list other than just shameless self-promotion? The point is, all this stuff is linked together so that, technologically, everything gets to market everything else, and automatically. For example, examine Figure 3.11, the day-job Web site, and you see links to books on Amazon, plus a flashing rollover button on the left labeled "Music," which links to Gavin's music Web site. Also, Gavin's blog links to the music Web site (the blog is about music), and the music sites all link to each other—and some of them mention Gavin's work as an author as well.

Gavin's day-job Web site and books on Amazon generate occasional consulting work for him. All the music Web sites have not yet produced paying work for Gavin, but he has engineered one or two recordings for other amateur indie musicians. This particular angle might be become more consistent, and could turn into occasional paying work, as Gavin goes through the process of writing the *Book: Internet Marketing for Musicians.*

All of Gavin's Internet sites are advertising his skills and talents. Sometimes people notice expert-level skills on the Internet, and people sometimes offer small amounts of cash to borrow those skills for a short time. That's the idea, anyway. For Gavin, that could be to do Oracle Database consulting work or to sing his songs at someone's wedding.

The essential point of mentioning personal revenue in this book is to demonstrate how you can capitalize on spin-offs, perhaps offering expert services to folks. Your blog and your Web sites are all showcases for past work, for your knowledge and talents, and also each talent for every other talent you may have. Use your Internet presence to help you find new jobs, new clients, new work, new things to do, and new friends. This concept can be applied to any skill.

SELF-PROMOTION

Self-promotion is really part and parcel of personal revenue, but it's more a process of establishing credibility than one of directly bringing in revenue. The real objective is to try to set yourself up as a going concern in the hope that you will bring in future revenue. You want to bring in revenue, but if nobody knows who you are, then they are unlikely to hire you or give you a contract that will bring some money in the door.

So, what kind of things can you do as a blogger, and how can you build a reputation for yourself online? What can you do to promote yourself?

> Note: Promotion is all about building your name in a community. Using the Internet, the scope of that community could be the city you live in and a population of thousands or millions. On other hand, your community could also be the global Internet population of hundreds of millions of people worldwide.

You can do the following things, preferably with some crossover into personal revenue (making some income), and there are surely further possibilities:

- *Community forums.* Moderating at forums gives you added exposure by making yourself, your name, and your skill set known.

- *Other blogs.* Read other people's blogs in your subject area. Not only can you learn something, but you get added exposure to other readers—through other blogs. And there is always something new to learn from other experts in your field.

- *Writing for others.* Industry sites and publications, both online and offline, are always looking for contributors.

- *Public speaking and presentations.* Opportunities at conferences for speaking engagements and presentations should always be taken if possible. These activities can sometimes pay well and, in addition, give you more promotional exposure.

- *Webinar hosting.* You can host Webinars. A Webinar is an online educational seminar, which often contains both audio and video components.

- *White papers and e-books.* These are both great ways to gain exposure for your skills.

- *Social networking.* Many people may not take social networks, such as MySpace and YouTube, too seriously from a business or non-artistic-field perspective. Take a look at Figure 3.14 and then read on.

Figure 3.14 shows that MySpace can be used to find A&R people throughout the world. What is an A&R person you might ask? A&R means Artists and Repertoire. This is a person who seeks talent, particularly for record labels. For musicians, access to this kind of information is worth its weight in gold. These people actively seek out, sign, and develop recording and performing acts—for both indie (independent, or minor) record labels and major labels.

Try following these steps for yourself:

1. Open up your browser.

2. Go to this Web site: www.myspace.com.

3. Click the Search link.

4. Scroll to the bottom part of the page.

5. Examine the contents of the Field spin control, under the Affiliation for Networking box.

**FIGURE 3.14: FINDING PEOPLE ON A
SOCIAL NETWORK WEB SITE.**

6. Pick one or two of the fields that people are in and examine the Sub Field and Role spin control options for each. Two specific fields of interest for readers of *How to Make Money with Your Blog* could be Marketing and Technology.

Note: The limitation of networking affiliation categories on MySpace is restricted to what people are prepared to declare about themselves. Quite often, people are attempting to network both commercially and socially, so their specific details are usually easy to find.

People do use social networking Web sites for commercial networking. MySpace, in particular, is used by all sorts of professionals for commercial networking, especially for anything in the artistic field. MySpace is also full of spam advertisers for all sorts of things. Even social networking Web sites have quite extensive appeal, because commercially, people are less likely to hide their skills. It is possible in the future that Web sites like MySpace may become a major tool for commercial networking.

If you're more into the professional networking side of things, check out LinkedIn at www.linkedin.com. This is one of the largest networking Web sites for professionals. It's really amazing to see how many people you can access in a short period of time by inviting people to join your network or by receiving invitations to network with others. You will need to cultivate relationships, though, because, unlike social networking opportunities, most of the folks in places such as LinkedIn are there for professional reasons and guard their contact information closely if they don't know you or you don't come recommended by a trusted friend. The LinkedIn Web site is shown in Figure 3.15.

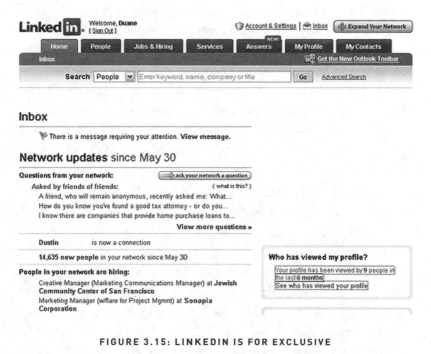

FIGURE 3.15: LINKEDIN IS FOR EXCLUSIVE
PROFESSIONAL NETWORKING.

ADDING ADS TO YOUR BLOG

This section takes you through the process of how to add advertisements to your blog for the first time.

Where to Start

We'll start by suggesting you stick with contextual systems such as Google and Yahoo if you are new to blogging and blog advertising. They are easy to set up, easy to use, offer decent tracking and stats, and pay regularly and on time (that said, *all* of those mentioned in this book tend to pay reliably). Google's system now offers the option of allowing image ads to be shown in the assigned ad spaces, so if you have to have images in those spaces, there you go.

If it sounds like we're not big fans of image-based ads . . . well, we're not. After almost a decade of using online ads to drive traffic to various Web sites, the simple fact is that text-based ads easily outperform image-based ads. Users know a picture is likely an ad, so they ignore it. Text, on the other hand, forces a user to read it if they want to interact with it. Placed carefully on your site, these text-based ads can generate handsome revenues for you.

Larger ad formats generally perform better than smaller ad sizes. So, if you plan to place an ad across the Web page, then choose to insert the 728×90 format, rather than the 468×60 format. The point here is that bigger is better, though you will have to balance this against your design goals, obviously, and the user's experience. Larger ads are more intrusive, as they physically take up more space. This may push content down lower on a page— "below the fold." Making a user scroll down a page to see content should never be your first choice. By striving to keep as much content as possible "above the fold" (viewable on the screen without the need to scroll), users can more effectively interact with your content and will likely appreciate the site more. Blogs get some relief in this regard, though, as readers are accustomed to having to scroll down at some point to read an entire post or article, but the point bears keeping in mind when laying out ads and navigation.

The rectangular-formatted ads tend to perform well when placed "inside" the page, meaning that you place them inside the actual text/article, like you would a picture.

Here are some common sizes, as recognized by the Internet Advertising Bureau:

Rectangles and Pop-Ups
300×250 (medium rectangle)
250×250 (square)
240×400 (vertical rectangle)
336×280 (large rectangle)
180×150 (rectangle)

Banners and Buttons
468×60 (full banner)
234×60 (half banner)
88×31 (microbar)
120×90 (button 1)
120×60 (button 2)
120×240 (vertical banner)
125×125 (square button)
728×90 (leaderboard)

Skyscrapers
160×600 (wide skyscraper)
120×600 (skyscraper)
300×600 (half-page ad)

Note: Specific ad formats for Google AdSense are shown in Figure 3.2.

Other sizes can easily be used, but you'll find that 99 percent of the ad programs you'll want to join use these sizes. More information can be found at www.iab.net. All units are measured in pixels, so 160 × 600 is 160 pixels wide and 600 pixels tall. It's also important to remember that you should not be loyal to any one size—test them and see which ones perform best on your blog, then use those sizes.

Though larger ads generally perform better than smaller ones, the price you pay is that a site with too many large ads might put off users. By taking the time to plan how and where you will place your ads, you can work them into the design of the page and have a workable solution for you and your users.

Most of the programs you'll want to sign up for have built-in limits on how many actual ads they will show on a page, so having too many ads should never be a real problem if you're running a system like Google AdSense. With Google, you are allowed a maximum of three ad units and one text link unit per page. Try for more, and the system will see what you're doing and turn off some ads.

Google, specifically, also has rules regarding pop-ups and pop-unders on your site. If any are detected, Google will most likely disable those ads. Your best bet when joining any advertising or affiliate program is to read every word of the agreement carefully. It will spell out in detail what you can and cannot do.

Ad Placement

There are many places you could turn to for this type of data, from specific white papers to historical data, but the easiest to find and understand is from Google itself. Google wants you to succeed and generate revenue with its ads on your site. It's a win-win situation. So, Google shares the following "heat map" with users to help them place ads in areas of the page that have been proven to perform in the past. It's not a guaranteed formula that works 100 percent of the time, but after studying reams of data, this is what Google suggests Webmasters do. We can say from personal experience, they're right on the money spots. Google AdSense suggests ad placements as shown in Figure 3.16.

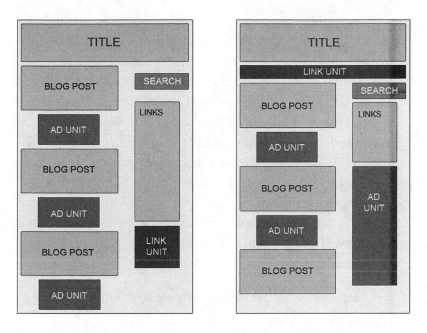

FIGURE 3.16: GOOGLE AD PLACEMENTS FOR BLOGS
From https://www.google.com/adsense/support/bin/snswer.py?answer=43869;
all Google images reproduced with the express permission of Google Inc.

Obviously, placing ads on a page takes planning and forethought. Your main concerns are as follows:

- Easy to see

- Close to content

- Easy to update or change

One really nice feature of blogs is their use of templates, or *themes*. A template is simply the "skin" that defines how the blog looks to users. It defines the colors and layout, basically. By changing the theme, it is possible to completely alter the colors of a blog, how the navigation looks, and where everything sits on the page itself. Thousands of themes exist for all of the platforms listed elsewhere in this book. Finding one you like is simple, installing it is simple, and using it is simple. The tricky bit comes in when you decide to customize a theme.

By deciding to place your ad in a specific spot on the page, you have, in many cases, opted to alter the theme itself. Most themes available today do not include defined spaces for ads. While this is changing daily as more themes come out with places for ads defined, you still may not like the overall theme for other reasons. The bottom line here is you'll likely want to edit some code at some point to get the ad you want integrated into the theme you want.

The bad news is you'll be "playing with code." The good news is you'll simply be pasting something in there, not changing anything already there. Here are some basic guidelines to follow to keep your blog's code safe:

- Make a copy of the file you'll be editing first—save this on your computer.

- Look for clues—if there's a search box in the header of your blog and you want an ad above it, look through the code to find something that references a search box. You'll often find the actual words in the code—in this case, *search box* could well appear.

- Paste the ad code into the spot you've chosen.

- Go the site, hit Refresh, and see where the ad is—if it's not in the correct spot, try again.

Following this trial-and-error patterns a few times will help you begin to understand how the blog is actually built.

All themes come with a name, so knowing which file to edit is as simple as knowing the name of your blog's theme. Platforms like WordPress make this very simple, and in any event, most theme authors place the name of the theme (and a link to themselves) at the bottom of the page.

You'll need to go onto the server hosting your blog at this point to find the file to edit. In most cases, you'll find the file you're after labeled as "header" (to install an ad along the top of your blog), and it will be in the folder with your theme's name.

Don't forget to make that backup copy at this point, before you start playing.

One word of caution when editing these files: we prefer to use a text editor such as UltraEdit. Most folks have access to MS Notepad on their computer, which can be used when editing these files. It's not likely to cause problems here, but other file types tend to have issues when saved in Notepad and uploaded to your server (like an .htaccess file). If you encounter a problem, try editing the file in another text editor. MS Word is not a text editor for our purposes.

Many bloggers tend to edit the header, sidebar, and footer files to include ads in them. The header is, obviously, the section near the top of the blog visually. It's not defined in any real visual way, but if you delete this file you'll see that there is obviously something missing.

The sidebar file is so called because it describes, usually, the section of content running vertically down one side of the blog. It could be on the left or right, and there may be more than one side-bar file. Trial and error in your particular theme will show you what's what. Or, if you have the time, you could try contacting the original theme designer to ask for directions about what's what.

It's important to note, though, that at this point your blog is still new, so feel free to experiment and learn on your own. The absolute worst that can happen is you'll need to reload a file you messed up. No biggie, jut another copy and paste maneuver.

After a while of editing various files, you'll become handy and really begin to have fun. Don't want the search box up top? Then move the code lower in the file to see what happens. In short order, you'll become familiar with the characters that signal the beginning and end of specific items in the code. The angle brackets (<>) brackets are used a lot, so if you're going to be copying some code, make sure you have one at the beginning and one at the end of what you have highlighted.

The front slash or forward slash character (/) is used a lot as well, and usually signifies the closing of a parameter. For example, code that looks like this means the text is blue:

```
<font color=blue>This font is blue.</font>
```

The expression is opened and defines the font between the triangular brackets as blue, then the whole expression is closed with </font>, thus defining which actual text should be blue.

Now, if you're using a system such as Google's Blogger to run your blog, things are much simpler to get going. Google's Blogger is ready-made to accommodate Google AdSense ads. You can try code from other programs, but don't be surprised if the system will run only AdSense ads.

Blogger makes choosing the theme and inserting ads very easy, so it's a great place to learn the basics and familiarize yourself with the concepts before breaking out on your own. The real downside is that customization is limited, and since the blog is not really on your own domain, it's not really a long-term solution for those seeking to build their blog into their own business. One great feature for the future, however, is that most of the bigger open-source platforms have an import feature that allows you to "go fetch" the content from the Blogger blog when you want to. So, starting with a blog at Blogger is a completely legitimate option for everyone, as upgrading later to one of the bigger stand-alone blog platforms is easily accomplished.

Blending ads

Ideally you'll want your ads to look as much a part of the site as possible. (See Figure 3.2.) Same font colors, same background colors, and so forth. The idea is simple—users tend to tune out things they perceive as ads. Making your ads look the same as the site itself reduces the chance of users thinking of them as ads. Text-based ads perform so much better than image-based ads because they can blend in, and users simply see the text, not pictures. If the text they see is appealing, they'll click it and you get paid.

Some folks see this as trickery, but the bottom line is, this is what it takes to generate the revenue. If you don't believe us, try running ads with the default colors set by Google and others, and watch your revenues tumble (or never really grow). The default colors from Google are some of the worst-performing colors combinations ever—unless your site happens to match those colors, that is. The best way to determine which color combination works best for your application is to test it for a week or so, then try another combo and watch the results. There are no rules about which works best, but ads blended into the site tend to outperform those that stand out.

There are two ways you can go about making the ads blend. You'll need to use the ad programs template system to change the colors, and using just this alone, you could keep trying colors until you find the perfect match. In some cases, this won't take you long at all. If the background is white, then using the color code *ffffff* will color the desired section white. Black is *000000* (zeros). When you get into shades of colors, though, it's a bit trickier. Now's the time to keep in mind one small fact: since the colors are actually numbers or letters or combinations of both, it's possible to replicate any color seen online perfectly. Here's the second way to figure out the colors and a couple of tricks to save you time.

You'll want to have the following piece of software downloaded and ready to use on your computer:

SnagIt (www.techsmith.com/download/trials.asp)

SnagIt is a handy item that lets you select any area on the screen you wish to capture. SnagIt offers a free trial, so it's just the ticket to getting started.

When you use something like this, your goal is to collect enough image data to allow you to determine the colors you're after. Your best bet is to capture a large enough area that includes some of the header, the main body, the sidebar, and some text from the blog. This will ensure you have a sample of almost all the colors on the blog, thus making it easier to blend in the ads.

You will also need image editing software to complete this step. Adobe Photoshop (older or newer doesn't really matter) or MacroMedia Fireworks are a couple of our favorites. Many others will work as well. If the program will show you a color code, it'll work for ourpurposes. The goal is to see the color as a number code.

The essence of this small project is as follows:

- You'll grab a snapshot of the page you want to blend the ad into.

- Using the image editing software, you'll determine the color code of the area you wish to match your ad to.

- By using the color code shown in the image editing software, you can make the background of your ad blend perfectly with the background color on the blog.

Figure 3.17 shows a screenshot of ads perfectly blended with a site's background.

You can see how the *Official Ford Canada Site* ad at the top, and the smaller *Free Moving Truck* and *Online Classified Ads* advertise-

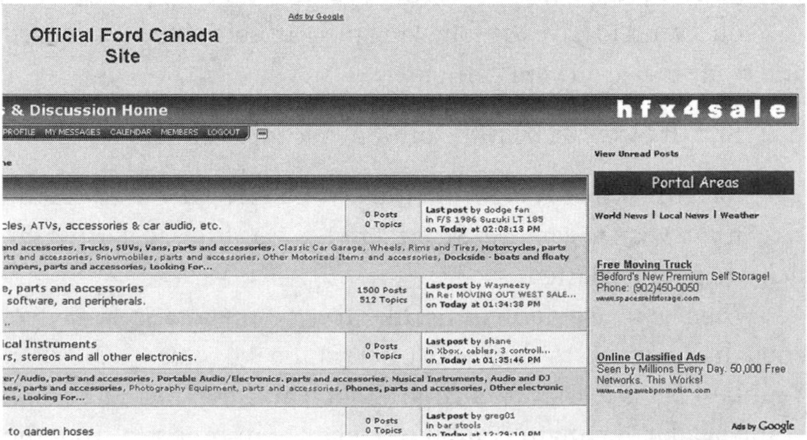

FIGURE 3.17: DEMONSTRATING SOME VERY WELL-BLENDED ADS.

ments are visible, yet appear to blend seamlessly with the background of the site. Though this example is from a community discussion forum, the concept is the same.

Now here's the step-by-step process used to blend ads:

- Select the page you want to match the ads to. For this example, we'll use www.blowupmyride.com, an automotive news blog.

- Use SnagIt to capture a portion of the screen—save this image on your computer, as shown in Figure 3.18.

- Use Photoshop to open the image and determine the background color you want to blend the ad with, as shown in Figure 3.19.

- Use the color code from Photoshop to update the ad code in, for example, Google AdSense, as shown in Figure 3.20.

- Place the ad into the blog space you've chosen, as shown in Figure 3.21.

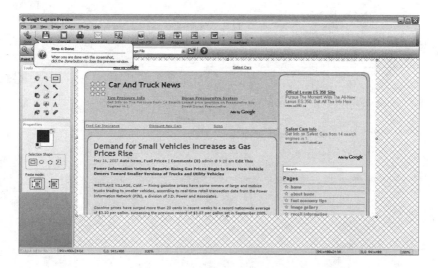

FIGURE 3.18: USING SNAGIT TO CAPTURE A SCREENSHOT.

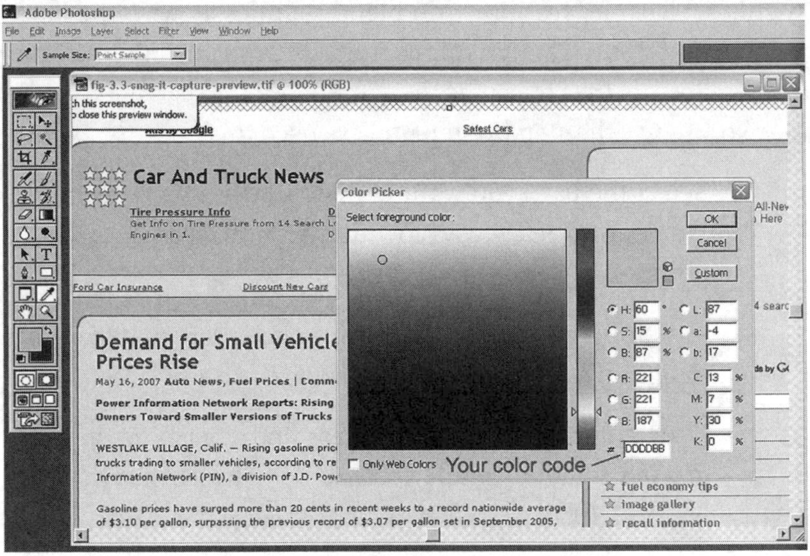

FIGURE 3.19: USING PHOTOSHOP TO DETERMINE A COLOR CODE.

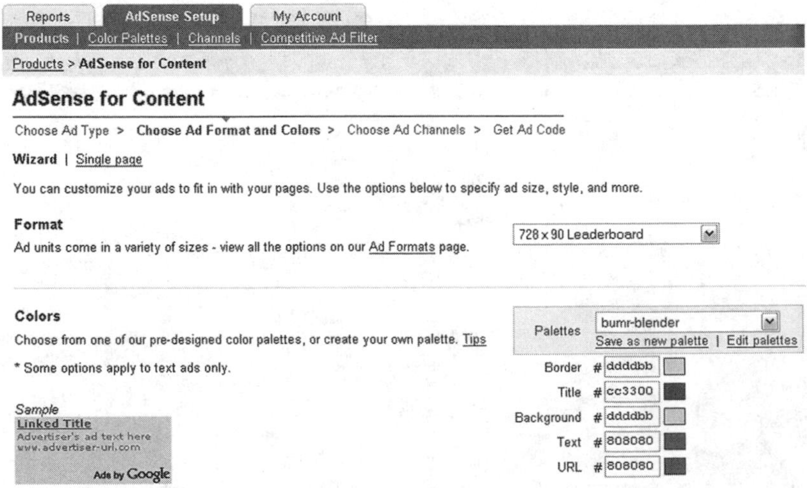

FIGURE 3.20: USING THE COLOR CODE IN ADSENSE.

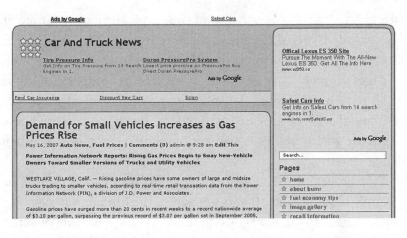

FIGURE 3.21: FULLY BLENDED ADS LIVE.

Inclusion of Ads

You will need to decide how you want to place ads into the page it-self early in the building process if you're going to alter a theme or template. One way to get ads into the page is to hard-code them in. This basically involves taking the ad code given to you by Google or another provider and placing it in the code of the page while you are building it. When you save and publish the page, the code goes live and (after a short delay) the ads will begin showing in the space into which you set the Google AdSense code. Make sure to match the ad size you want to show (and thus the code you get from Google or another provider) with the space provided in your tem-plate. Dropping a 728 × 90 ad into a 468 × 60 space will not work. It'll still show, but it will obviously be problematic, and most of the ad will remain invisible. The biggest drawback to hard-coding ads into the page is that to change an ad means editing the page. If you plan to always use only one ad platform, say Google AdSense, then this is fine. The ads themselves will vary as Google rotates differ-ent advertisers in and out, so fresh ads will always appear. But you are limited to seeing only Google's ads with this option.

A better way to get ads into a page is to use what's known as an "include." This nifty little item allows you to use a separate "document" that holds only the ad code for a given space and will be "included" anywhere the include code sits. The benefits are clear. You must edit only one item to change ads across hundreds of pages at once. This is less of a concern for bloggers, though, as, generally speaking, blog platforms consist of only a small number of actual pages. So you'll only be installing code on a few pages anyway, whether it's ad code, include code, or any other code.

The *header* file mentioned earlier in this book can be used as an example of an include. It appears across the top of every page on your blog, so anything installed in this file will appear everywhere.

If you do wish to use includes, your server platform will dictate which form of include code you use, as Windows- and Linux-based servers differ slightly in how they handle this action. The end result is the same, though. By constructing individual includes, one for each ad size you want to show, you can maximize the ads placed across your Web site. If you find advertisers who want to pay to show ads on your site, you simply replace the code in the include from Google (or another provider) with the information on where the advertisers ads reside (this will depend on whether you are hosting the ad or the advertiser is; either way it's a simply URL— the direct path to the advertiser's ad itself) and you're finished. It takes less than five minutes from logging on to your server's administration system to seeing the changes.

Here's a sample of code used in a Linux environment:

```php
<?php include('includes/test_header.php'); ?>
```

In this example, we're including a file named "test_header.php." It can be called .html and it'll still work. This file resides in a folder on the server called "includes." Thus, any time we want to update the header on this Web site, we simply go to the folder for the includes, open the file called "test_header.php," and make our changes. When uploaded to the server again and saved, the changes will be live across the entire site. It's important to note that each character and space must be as shown here for this to work properly. You can change the folder and file names, but everything else should remain as shown.

For Windows-based folks, this code should work:

```
<!--#include virtual="/Headers_Toolbar/
headers/header.html"-->
```

It will require you to build your pages setup to use "virtual includes" or server side includes (SSIs), which is a setting you'll need to make in your editing software of choice.

Another option for more advanced users is ad serving software. These platforms allow you to load many different ads of the same size and show them in rotation in the same space on your blog. This is very handy if you have a series of related blogs that are each on a slightly different topic. An example would be a series of automotive blogs, each talking about a select brand. You may wish to show ads across all of your blogs from the same advertiser, and this is easily set up in ad serving software. You'll still need to install the "ad invocation code" in the spaces reserved for ads on your blog. This code is what actually goes and fetches the ad each time a page on your blog is refreshed or loaded.

On many of the blogs, Web sites, and forums run by Duane, the ad invocation code looks like this:

```php
<?php
  if (@include(getenv('DOCUMENT_ROOT').'/
phpAdsNew-2.0.7/phpadsnew.inc.php')) {
    if (!isset($phpAds_context))
    $phpAds_context = array();
    $phpAds_raw = view_raw ('zone:1', 0, '',
    '', '0', $phpAds_context);
    echo $phpAds_raw['html'];
  }
?>
```

It is generated by an ad serving platform called PHPAdsNew. The newest version is called OpenAds (www.openads.org). It's the same platform, though, and being open-source, it's free to anyone wishing to download a copy. It'll take some know-how to set it up yourself, but there is an active support community you can turn to, and you could likely even arrange to pay someone to install this for you.

The basic process when using as serving software, free or otherwise, is the same:

1. Install the ad invocation code in the space you want the ad to appear in—make sure your sizes match.

2. Upload a banner into the ad software.

3. Follow the instructions on how to set up a campaign and assign banners to selected spaces.

That's it. In an afternoon, you can have this installed, set up, and know how to use it. It'll take someone new to the entire concept a bit longer, but again, help is available. OpenAds community discussion forums can be found at forum.openads.org.

Using ad serving software is fairly advanced in its needs and setup, but the flexibility it offers you down the road makes it worth looking into. Out of the gate, however, keeping this simpler by just placing the code from your ad program of choice (Google, Yahoo, MSN, etc.) is just as effective.

The bottom line is that when planning your ads and placing them into the pages, it's a safe bet you will be making some changes down the road. It's part of the nature of testing to see what generates the most revenue for you on a given blog with a given audience.

Getting the right ads, with the right look, into the right spots takes some time and testing. The information provided here should have you pretty close to having the right ads, with the right look, and in the right spots—right from the start. It's always best to test, test, test and refine on your own. If you have the time and knowledge, you really can build a series of revenue-generating blogs, thereby creating a whole new career for yourself—managing your blogs from home each day.

SUMMARY

As you can now see, there are many potential ways to generate revenue from your blog. Whether you are selling products directly or simply selling ad space, avenues exist to help you maximize your opportunities:

- *Use resources wisely.* The resources mentioned in this chapter are not the only ones available to you. They are, however, some of the best places to start.

- *Do your research.* Make sure you exercise due diligence when deciding which providers and programs to use. Make certain to read all their rules carefully, and if you have a question, drop them a line—they'll answer you.

- *Be transparent.* If you are receiving compensation for things you write about a product or Web site, let your readers know this. Your credibility may suffer otherwise.

- *Blend, blend, blend.* If you're integrating ads into your blog, do your best to blend them in thoroughly. Be sure to read each program's guidelines for limitations on the number of ads you can use. Then get cracking on making those ads look like part of the blog.

- *Test, test, test!* You need to test everything. Certain color combinations of ads may work better than others. Different programs may generate more money in the same space as others. Your readers may respond better to one type or size of ad than to others. Continual testing will keep you on top of the revenue curve.

We cannot stress this final point enough: *build relationships.* Build relationships with both advertisers and your readers. Always strive for a balance that works for both parties. Without readers, advertisers will evaporate. Without advertisers, there's no revenue.

Strike the right balance, and you'll see steady revenues and happy readers—the ideal combination.

If you are selling your own personal services, be an active member within your own online community. It's an excellent way to establish your credibility and credentials . . . and to generate business leads as well.

MANAGING YOUR
BLOG

WHAT'S IN THIS CHAPTER?

This chapter is all about what you should be doing on a daily basis to keep your blog up and running, as available and visible as possible, and making you as much advertising revenue as you can. That's an ideal, but it makes a good goal to aim for. And that goal is realistic if you are patient and don't expect to make millions. Some people make millions, but they are a rarity. There is no reason you shouldn't. However, other bloggers do make a living by blogging—that is certainly a possible goal. Realistically, to earn a few hundred dollars a month would be considered successful, and to earn a few thousand dollars a month would probably require you to add in some advertising costs up front.

A few of the tasks involved in managing your blog would be things like making sure spam and obnoxious comments are visible as briefly as possible. You also need to make sure you treat blogging as a business if you expect to earn advertising revenue and expect advertising people to take you seriously. Most important are feeds that allow you to automatically get repeat visitors to your blog. If your blog is interesting and useful enough, then readers will subscribe. You need to provide the facility for readers to subscribe by providing them an online feed.

MODERATING COMMENTS AND SPAM MANAGEMENT

Since your goal for your blog is to grow its usage, you'll eventually end up with readers. Those readers will often desire to comment on something you've posted. Whether it's to agree with it or disagree with it is irrelevant. What matters is that they are engaged, and you now need to figure out how to deal with this.

Many blog platforms offer you blanket controls to manage comments in a default manner. You can choose to allow them, disallow them, or hold them for review by the administrator. Using WordPress as an example, you can then override these blanket controls on a post-by-post basis, should you so choose.

This offers you the ability to set the default to moderate all comments (meaning the admin must approve or disapprove them), which will help control spam and yet still select individual posts or articles on which to allow comments.

You do want to encourage comments, though, so don't think

that setting the default to ignore all comments is the ticket to controlling spam. While it may be true such a setting will effectively control most spam, it will also kill off all legitimate commentary made by your readers. Most users of blogs enjoy the interaction of adding their comments. They're not expecting to start a conversation with anyone (that's what posting forums are for, after all), but if you never allow reader's comments to appear, they feel cut out of the loop.

Additionally, you should remember that an engaged readership will help create useful, unique content for you, and that's something you definitely want to encourage.

So you'll need to find the balance between blocking spam, providing yourself time to manage things, and allowing user's comments to go live. You must find this balance. Too much time from you, and you'll feel as though the project is taking all your time. This thinking will lead you to ignore the blog eventually, and it will languish. Too many spam comments, and readers won't enjoy the blog. As well, since most spam on blogs is the sort that drops links, your blog will now be linking to many sites you'd never choose to associate with. Adult sites, gambling sites, and more are often found to be trying to drop links on blogs. The more popular the blog, the more likely they'll be as a target for spammers.

Spammers are after two things:

1. Traffic from your blog

2. PR from your page where the link appears

If you make a post on a hot topic and your blog gets noticed for this post, you'll see an influx in traffic as readers find you and explore. Spammers are happy to exploit hot-topic issues. You've done the work of writing an article that is noticed enough to generate some traffic. The spammer then tries for a link from the comments area below the article in hope that the traffic you're enjoying will spill over to the spammer via his or her link.

That second reason is why you'll often see comment spam on older posts. It takes time for a post to accumulate some PageRank value of its own. During this aging process, spiders and spammers generally leave a post alone if they're fishing for a higher ranking. But when the post gets some rank of its own, the comments start. Spammers try to set up a one-way link from your page to theirs. By doing this, they leverage your PageRank value to help support their own ranking.

Spammers often try to make their post look like a real comment by copying a portion of your original article or post and submitting it as their comment. This type of comment spam is usually managed by robots programmed to find blogs on certain topics or with specific characteristics.

Therefore, a blog in a popular topic, like search optimization and online marketing, that also has a decent PageRank rating from Google (such as a 5 or 6 out of 10), will attract spammers. They usually practice "drive-by" spamming, and you'll see it come in waves. For days at a time, spam will appear on old posts, seemingly at random. You'll remove it, or disallow it if you're moderating all comments, and later that day it's back again. After a while, that particular robot will move on to another domain in search of success.

In the fight against spam, there's one surefire solution. There's one thing you can throw at the problem that will absolutely make a difference: *time*.

If you set the comments to allow all, you'll be constantly surfing your own site trying to track down comments and remove ones you don't want. If the comments are set to block all, users may become frustrated and your traffic may suffer. For many people, setting the blog platform to "moderate all" comments is the best solution. This allows users to post comments, and you get to decide which ones will actually go live after you've reviewed them.

It takes time to wade through the comments pending approval, but better this than your blog suddenly linking to adult Web sites and offending your users.

When you see a comment with a link in it awaiting approval, there are a few things you can do:

- Read it. Just take a look through what is written. Spiders write differently than humans. In fact, spiders often just copy a portion of the text *you* wrote originally, while humans usually try to make a comment of some sort. By getting in the habit of scanning through the comments themselves, you'll quickly become adept at picking out the real comments from the spam.

- You will also see the URL the commenter is trying to link to. Click it. Where does it take you? If it's someone else's personal blog, it's your call whether you want to leave the link to them in place. Generally, it's good form to leave it in place, but always remember that your site is judged by the sites it links to. If the link takes you somewhere you don't want to be associated with, just delete it.

- You could also choose to defer the decision until later, thus leaving the comment pending. You can see it in the admin section, but readers will not see it on the site.

- Often, the software you're using will have captured the IP address of the commenter, and this information will prove useful if you ever need it to ban a spammer. If your system is set up to require commenters to join your blog as a registered user, you may also have their e-mail address—another useful item to know.

You might want to try setting up a process, or checklist, that you follow when evaluating a comment:

1. Does it appear to be real? (Does it read like a human wrote it?)

2. Does it link to a real site? (Is the site real, or is it merely a page full of links or other junk?)

3. Is the site acceptable by my standards?

4. Does this same Web site have links in other comments on my blog? (You may choose to allow only one link per domain from your Web site.)

That short list should get you started. If the answers look good, then allow the comment to go live and the link to stand. If something seems amiss to you, delete the comment and move on.

One handy feature is the ability to have your blog automatically e-mail any pending comments to you. This will save you from having to log into your admin section to manage the comments. The blog will automatically e-mail to you the details and links to allow you to accept, delete, or leave the comment as pending. Clicking, for example, the delete link will take you immediately into your blog's admin section and into the exact page needed to manage that actual comment. The top of the page will ask you if you are sure you want to delete the comment. By clicking the "Yes" button, the comment is removed from the database.

It's a very handy way to manage comments on multiple blogs, as each one will send an e-mail to your inbox for every comment posted. Using the preceding short checklist, you can quickly go through the list to manage them all and allow the real comments to stand and the spam to be removed.

Blocking Spammers

At some point, you will face a situation where a persistent commenter or spammer just won't leave your blog alone. It's starting to take more time to moderate that person's spam, and you're frustrated. What do you do?

You dig into the admin area of your blog platform; you look for the section that allows you to deal with your users; and you start setting up the blockades. The IP address captured as such spammers logged their comment can be used to block them in the future. Same goes for the e-mail they submitted if you made them register before commenting. Blocking both will effectively silence spammers from coming back under those identities. They may well come back under a different IP or with a different e-mail address, but you do what you can when you need to.

One word of warning about blocking IP addresses. While this can be an effective and powerful way to block unwanted users from accessing your site or to disable commenting from them, IP addresses are not universally individualized. If you are online from home, most Internet service providers (ISPs) will mask your actual IP address (the one from your computer) to protect you. The ISP then assigns to you one of its "anonymous" IP addresses. It's this anonymous IP address that your blog software will see and capture.

This isn't an issue until you realize that the same so-called anonymous IP address may be in use by hundreds or thousands of users being serviced by that same ISP. So, blocking an IP address in this case could result in many users being blocked from commenting on your site.

If you choose to block only by e-mail addresses, be careful. Most spammers will simply invest in something that looks like an e-mail address to register in the first place. This makes it very easy for them to simply try another made-up e-mail address if one gets blocked.

So, where does this leave you for effectively controlling spam? Back to investing a bit of your own time in running your blog. Running a blog, as we've mentioned elsewhere, will take time. There is no getting around it. Take heart, however, as new blogs tend to be less frequent targets for spammers. New blogs simply have less to offer them. Established bloggers will have figured out their ways of effectively dealing with spam.

GIVING PEOPLE FREE STUFF

In any business, particularly when it uses the Internet, people just love free stuff! Remember that one. Offer people something for free, and you will attract traffic to your site. Then again, free things have been available on the Internet for so many years that it is no longer an exception. However, not offering any freebies could make your blog exceptional from a negative perspective—so beware.

What can you as a blogger offer for free? You are doing it right now—it's your blog. Information, your expertise, and valuable experience in whatever topic your blog covers. Make sure you blog about something you know a lot about. It could be anything at all. You might want to avoid religion and politics. Upsetting people will not generate advertising revenue. No matter which way you cut it, these topics will upset someone somewhere.

Your ultimate objective is advertising revenue. Freebies will certainly help. Offer people things for free in order to persuade people to read your postings, visit your blog again and again, and maybe eventually click on your ads. In some industries, offering freebies over and above your blog is easy. In the music industry, you can offer free CDs, free T-shirts, free MP3 downloads (free music), cheap concert tickets—the list goes on and on. As long as you spark an emotional response in people, they will respond. Free offerings can help, as they inspire a smiley or "oh goody goody" feeling in people. It also helps if your freebies are not junk.

Offering free things on a blog is a little more subtle than the blatant product offering of free CDs and cut-rate concert tickets— these items are all physical things that a person can see, touch, hold, use, listen to, and so on. Information is somewhat more intangible in that people absorb data. It is also much less physically taxing to put a CD in a CD player and then sit and listen while relaxing. Using information on how to make your blog more profitable requires reading, concentrating while reading (not relaxing), and then going to a computer and sitting for hours trying to figure out exactly how to make all this stuff work on your own blog.

Freebies you can give away via your blog can be things like news feeds and weather feeds. If you like to read the news and keep abreast of global developments, a news feed from the Cable News Network (CNN) would suffice. Perhaps 90 percent of your blog readership lives in tornado alley in Kansas, or in South Florida in the hurricane belt. In that case, an emergency weather warning feed could attract people to your blog. You could also offer special discounts on books. In one of my MySpace blog entries, I stated that every time I publish a book, publishers send me 10 free copies. I offered to give the books away. Nobody responded. The question is, why? Well, I placed the free-books offer on the MySpace profile for my band, The EZPowell Band, which is music-related. The books' topics are all computer-related, including things like Oracle Database, SQL Server, and database modeling. In short, rock music does not mix well with Oracle Database Administration and relational database design textbooks. There was a slight context clash there. That was of course many eons ago when my understanding of Internet marketing and promotion was infantile, to say the least. I am much, much better at it now. Sometime in the future, when I have time, I will start up and maintain technical blogs on various topics. One of those topics will be audio engineering; another topic will be computer engineering. But mixing the two is something I will not do. Because it's not very bright!

TREATING IT LIKE A BUSINESS

Given that you're busy reading a book called *How to Make Money with Your Blog*, you might want to be treating your blogging activities as a business. In other words, you are trying to turn a profit with your blog and, essentially, turn a profit with your time. The amount of profit you consider adequate may relate directly to how much you think your time is worth. If, for example, you're a pediatrician earning $250,000 per year, it might seem pointless to you to invest an hour a day, day after day, ad infinitum, in a blog that earns $50 a month. Of course, you're probably still going to be a blogger if you like it. Or you could be inventive with your ad space on your blog and advertise for charities. For example, Figure 4.1 shows my MySpace page for my band, the EZPowell band. It doesn't have to be about money.

Figure 4.2 shows another MySpace page. No, this is not a blog, but you get the point—nonprofit causes are being promoted. And as a side issue, promoting nonprofit causes is a sensible long-term promotional activity as well.

If it's a business, then treat it like one. Take it seriously if you expect others to take you seriously. You most especially want your advertisers to take you seriously because, as a blogger, you are looking to publish their ads to the world at large. Put promotional and

FIGURE 4.1: USING PROMOTIONAL SPACE ONLINE
FOR GOOD CAUSES.

FIGURE 4.2: DEDICATION TO USING PROMOTIONAL SPACE ONLINE IS COMMON.

profit-making incentives ahead of fun. As already stated, do bear in mind that supporting charities and nonprofit organizations is a good marketing tactic—it makes you look good and gives you yet more exposure. The charities benefit from the publicity as well. From a personal perspective, if I had the public's attention I would most certainly use my influence to encourage donations to the causes I feel are the most worthy of attention. But that's just me.

> Note: Blogging is addictive. So are social networks. If you're a musician, don't forget to practice. If you have a day job, make sure you get enough sleep, and don't neglect those you love the most. And if you're a blogger reading a book *called How to Make Money with Your Blog*, don't forget that you want your audience to support your blogging fun time by clicking on your blog ads.

Focus on those tasks, the blogs, and even the postings within your blogs that will either generate revenue for you or perform promotions. And promotions you do should ultimately generate revenue for you—at the very least, they should have that objective. If it's a business, treat it as such. It has to turn a profit. Otherwise, you are running a tax loss with nothing you can write off, and if you try to write off your time, then you will probably be breaking a few tax laws. You will realize you have a problem only when someone from the IRS knocks on your door, and you may discover that person is more intelligent than you are. Otherwise, you are running a nonprofit just for fun, and everyone has to make a living and pay the bills—even you.

So, you can promote, you can talk, you can polish your ego, and you can make your conscience and your opinions known. I had a political blog once—it made no advertising revenue whatsoever. Trust me—nobody's interested. If you have to be extremely controversial to attract attention, you might get angry people responding with commentary. Angry people definitely don't click on your ads. All that freedom of expression might very well be far removed from the focus of generating revenue with your blog. Once again, for the umpteenth time, that is probably why you are reading a book called *How to Make Money with Your Blog*. Focus on the tasks at hand:

- Promoting to generate revenue

- Generating revenue

BEING REALISTIC ABOUT TRAFFIC LEVELS

One critical point to talk about is being realistic about your traffic levels. It would be great to think that because you went live with your blog, people will flock to it. We cover ways to promote your blog elsewhere in this book, so now it's time to look at the reality of traffic volumes.

First and foremost—don't guess. Get yourself a dedicated analytics package. Google offers Google Analytics free to anyone, but make sure you read any rules and guidelines for any restrictions.

Whether you are using an analytics package that came with your hosting solution, Google Analytics, other solutions such as

ClickTracks, or even high-end applications such as WebTrends, it's not the platform that's valuable, it's the data it provides.

Your main concerns should be the following items of information:

- Visits

- Unique visitors

- Page views

- Time on site

And, in detail:

- *Visits.* This tells you how many people came to the blog during the selected period of time.

- *Unique visitors.* This is a count of those who came to you for the very first time. This number is included in the visits count, but is useful on its own to give you an idea of how many new people your blog is attracting. This number relies on cookies being enabled on users' computers, so if individuals have their cookies turned off, they will appear as a "unique visitor" every time they show up. Don't sweat this, though, as most folks have cookies enabled these days.

- *Page views.* This is a count of how many pages your visitors have viewed. It's a total count, so bigger is better. Blogs tend to have lower page view counts compared to Web sites, because more content is readable on the main page of a blog, in general. To encourage page views, look at using the option that allows you to insert a small link to "Read more" or "Read the entire story." Doing this encourages blog readers to click on the link to read the full story, thus increasing your page view count.

- *Time on site.* This is great stat to help you understand your readers' behavior. If they are spending 10 minutes or so reading on your blog, you should be extremely happy. Obviously the longer they are there, the more engagement they have with your blog. Keep in mind, though, that shorter-duration visits may simply reflect the fact that they come daily to read the newest posts then move on quickly.

In the end, it's your traffic volumes that will help you understand how you are doing. With increased traffic comes increased potential for revenue. More readers mean more page views, which in turn mean more ads shown (more ad impressions). Showing large volumes of ad impressions may be the key to gaining your blog entry into the larger advertising networks, too.

When the time comes to crunch the data, be honest. If you're seeing only 100 visits a month and 300 page views a month, don't worry about it. As we've pointed out elsewhere, all things take time. If you keep providing good, unique content, more readers will come, visits and page views will rise, and revenues will increase. Fudging the numbers is a shortcut to disappointment. Advertisers will quickly know whether you can deliver what you say you can.

SPREADING THE WORD WITH FEEDS

This heading begs two questions: (1) What is *spreading the word*? And (2) What's a *feed*? Spreading the word is telling lots and lots of people about your blog. Why? Because you want them to go to your blog, read it, say nice things about you, and tell lots of other people. Somewhere in that process, lots of people click on your ads, and you get to buy some more coffee, and you can stay awake a little longer, and keep blogging.

To answer the second question, a feed is similar to that little ticker thing you see at the bottom of your TV screen on some news and weather channels. And it is called a *ticker*. TV tickers were likely developed originally for stock price feeds, and now they contain everything from news to weather to stock price updates and the price of tomatoes in Wollongong, New South Wales, Australia. Of course, if you don't live in Australia that's an uninteresting feed. Feeds are no longer just a thing for television and the stock market; there are online as well as offline (on TV) feeds.

A modern online feed can be anything and everything. When you find a feed you like, then you can add it to your blog if you want. That feed could contain stock prices for Acme Tools Inc., the latest news headlines on BBC America or CCN, a local weather report, the price of some kind of weird vegetable in Diego Garcia (that's Outer Mongolia to the English), or it could be a feed of your blog! Yes, you can really, really create a thing to allow people to automatically see any changes to *your* blog on their own blog, in their e-mail, on their Web sites, or even on their computer desktop. How's that for neat?

So, you can add functionality to your blog that will allow your readers and fans (other bloggers) to subscribe to your feed (your blog). They will then get some kind of a direct notification whenever you add something new to your blog. With any luck, they will read your new entry and click on one of your ads—and you get to stay awake a little longer because you can now afford to buy that extra cup of coffee, and blog some more.

Syndicating Globally with RSS

Really Simple Syndication (RSS) is a specialized programming language used to broadcast information in a consistent format across the Internet. Chapter 2 very briefly discussed where on the Internet to submit your blog or RSS feed. This section in this chapter describes how to create that RSS feed.

What Is Syndication?
First of all, *syndication* is a process of taking a specific production of some kind, such as a TV or radio show, from a local station and

broadcasting over a multitude of stations all over a large country such as the United States. Generally, this makes huge amounts of money for artists because it distributes that production to an entire population, which in the United States is hundreds of millions of consumers.

Syndication over the Internet is essentially broadcasting Internet content to the entire Internet. RSS syndication is not exactly broadcasting to everyone on the Internet, but rather it makes specific Web pages available for broadcast to the entire Internet. Essentially, an RSS document is a feed that Internet users can add to their own blogs and Web pages. If a change occurs to the Web page that a feed is pointed to, then indication of that change is, in effect, broadcast—because all pointers to the feed (contained in people's blogs) will read the RSS document every time the blog containing the feed loads or refreshes. So, an RSS feed is not an automatic instantaneous broadcast, but it is rather ready to be broadcast on request.

Syndication and RSS

RSS is the syndicate because it is the vehicle used to distribute the Web content. Thus, RSS is like a computerized distributor of information across the Internet.

How is Internet syndication achieved using RSS? RSS is a standardized computer programming language written in an Internet scripting (or programming) language called eXtensible Markup Language (XML). XML is also a globally accepted standard. That means that everybody who writes XML will do so the same way and that, ultimately, all computers reading XML will be able to do something useful with it.

> Note: A standardized computer programming language is a language that should be identical on all computers, regardless of operating system, vendor, tool, and so on. The word *should* is used because there is no guarantee of this, and individual vendors often attempt to add their own vari-

ations to standards. Vendors sometimes do this kind of thing because either their products are substandard or they are trying to monopolize the market for themselves, regardless of the needs of consumers.

RSS is a language used to feed out Internet-published information that is frequently changed. Blogs frequently have new postings. Other items included in this frequent-change category are things like headline news items, weather reports, and even podcasts.

Note: A podcast is most commonly a collection of MP3 music files. All of these files are stored at a specific Internet Web site. This Web site is the address on the Internet from which the music files are fed (the feed). Whenever a music file is updated and someone on the Internet has a copy of that MP3 file, then the new copy is automatically downloaded.

RSS, feed Web sites, and a feed on a blogger's blog, work in concert to implement automated downloads and indicators of new content on other people's blogs. In short, it's automated and is much more efficient than millions of individual bloggers and blog readers having to fetch updates manually. They won't do it, and you will lose out on thousands of potential readers. Using a feed, your linked content is about a million times more likely to be noticed, and possibly read. An additional program called a *feed reader* aggregates content from one or more feed sources. A perfect example of an aggregator is iTunes, which aggregates music files from multiple sources and then automatically feeds it out to subscribing podcasters.

SYNDICATION IN ACTION

The word *subscription* is commonly used to describe an Internet user's preference to automatically "hear about" any changes made to feed content. Figure 4.3 is another one of my MySpace profiles

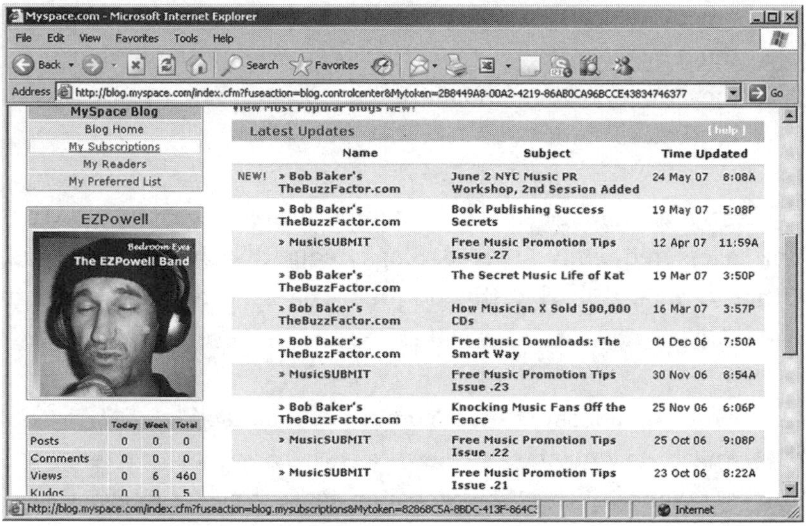

FIGURE 4.3: SUBSCRIPTIONS TO OTHER PEOPLE'S BLOGS ON MYSPACE AUTOMATICALLY FEED ME INFORMATION ABOUT OTHERS.

showing messages received by me that indicate new postings to blogs belonging to other MySpace users.

As shown in Figure 4.3, I have opted to receive new blog posting messages from various other MySpace profiles because I have subscribed to their feeds (their blogs in their MySpace profiles). Also, in Figure 4.3 you can see multiple blog posting notices from multiple MySpace profiles. MySpace is effectively acting as the content aggregator for its user's blogs, because new postings are sent to me from all MySpace blogs to which I am currently subscribed. The screen you see in Figure 4.3 is the MySpace internal blog feed reader.

On the other side of the coin, Figure 4.4 shows my blog readers—those who subscribe to my MySpace Blog.

The MySpace user shown in Figure 4.4 will receive a message in her equivalent subscriptions screen (see Figure 4.3) of any new posting I make to my MySpace Blog.

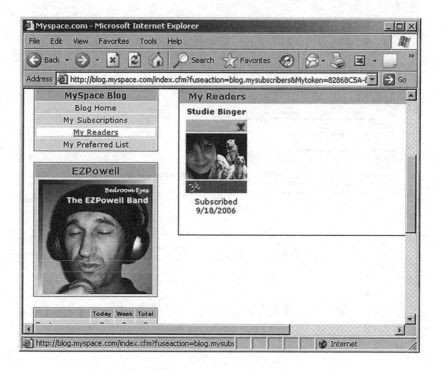

FIGURE 4.4: SUBSCRIPTIONS TO MY BLOG ON MYSPACE

AUTOMATICALLY FEED INFORMATION ABOUT MYSELF

TO OTHERS.

Effectively, MySpace syndicates and aggregates all blog feeding within its population of 200+ million users. The process of RSS is contained within the MySpace software. It may or may not be built with RSS. However, MySpace users can also publicize their blogs beyond the boundaries of the MySpace user population and send their RSS feeds to search engines, including Google or Yahoo. MySpace allows its users direct access to an RSS programming language file, which they can then use to broadcast everywhere else on the Internet, as shown in Figure 4.5.

When sending an RSS feed to somewhere like Google, you don't submit the entire RSS file. You submit only the link to the file, which in the case of Figure 4.5 is the blog address of the user on MySpace.

```
<?xml version="1.0" encoding="UTF-8" ?>
- <rss xmlns:itunes="http://www.itunes.com/DTDs/Podcast-1.0.dtd" version="2.0">
  - <channel>
      <title>http://www.ezpowell.com</title>
      <link>http://blog.myspace.com/theezpowellband</link>
      <description />
      <language>en-us</language>
      <pubDate />
      <generator>blog.myspace.com</generator>
      <ttl>60</ttl>
    - <image>
        <url>http://a744.ac-images.myspacecdn.com/01540/34/75/1540315743_m.jpg</url>
        <title>http://www.ezpowell.com</title>
        <link>http://blog.myspace.com/theezpowellband</link>
      </image>
      <itunes:author>EZPowell</itunes:author>
      <itunes:subtitle />
    - <itunes:owner>
        <itunes:name>EZPowell</itunes:name>
      </itunes:owner>
      <itunes:image href="http://a744.ac-
        images.myspacecdn.com/01540/34/75/1540315743_m.jpg" />
      <itunes:category text="Audio Blogs" />
    </channel>
  </rss>
  <!-- onRequestEnd -->
```

FIGURE 4.5: MYSPACE PROVIDES THE RSS CODING OF EACH
USER'S BLOG.

A good example of a podcaster is iTunes, which aggregates many radio stations into a single podcast available to the global Internet population. Now that's an aggregator! That's content! That's syndication in action! RSS and blogging are only a very small part of the amount and diversity of information fed automatically over the Internet.

RSS Documents Are Programmed in XML

XML has proven over time to be a wonderful and versatile new invention. XML syntax essentially stores both data and metadata into a single file. Data is information about a particular topic such as a customer's name and address. Metadata is the data about the data, which is the definition containers for the data, such as the definition for customers (the customer table) and the fields containing the customer details. What this means, ultimately, is that an XML document is a database all by itself—nothing else is needed from a technical perspective.

In reality, the application of XML is an extremely rich environment. XML has been used to both define and build environments, in fact even to build new languages and definitional structures for all sorts of things. These things range from Native XML databases to applications and industries of all kinds. Just so you get the full picture and scope of the uses of XML, Figure 4.6 shows a smattering of the implementations of XML.

The other good thing about RSS and and the fact that it is constructed using XML is that it can be embedded into Web pages. After all, XML is a Web page language originally, just like HTML. So RSS can be executed directly in your browser.

XML SYNTAX IS ROOTED IN HTML

The roots of XML construction are based on the syntax of something called Hypertext Markup Language (HTML). So, to gain an understanding of RSS, it is best to have a very brief understanding of HTML first, then progress to XML, and finally to RSS.

HTML consists of tags and simple displayed text. Tags are delineated by the < and the > characters. The < character starts a tag definition, and the > character ends a definition. In the following example, the <B> tag dictates that text after it will be displayed as

Accounting XML	Food XML	Open Office XML
Address XML	Geospatial XML	Photo XML
Advertising XML	Government XML	Physics XML
Astronomy XML	Healthcare XML	Publishing XML
Building XML	Human Resources XML	Real Estate XML
Chemistry XML	Human XML	Telecommunications XML
Computing Environment XML	Instruments XML	Topic maps XML
Construction XML	Insurance XML	Trade XML
Content Syndication XML	Legal XML	Translation XML
Customer Information XML	Localization XML	Travel XML
Education XML	Manufacturing XML	Universal Business Language (UBL)
Electronic Data Interchange (EDI) XML	Math XML	Universal Data Element Framework (UDEF)
Finance XML	News XML	

FIGURE 4.6: SOME OF THE APPLICATIONS AND INDUSTRY-SPECIFIC XML VOCABULARIES.

bold, and the "</B>" tag closes the <B> tag, thus switching off bold font:

```
This is <B>bold</B> text.
```

Note: HTML text not contained within tag delimiters is just displayed as text without further interpretation by your browser, with the exception of some specific functionality control characters.

The preceding text is HTML code and can be saved to an HTML file, which has an html or htm extension. The HMTL file is then loaded into a browser, as shown in Figure 4.7.

As shown in Figure 4.7, the HTML tags are not visible in the browser. HTML is not strict. There are some points to note about HTML:

- An opening tag does not explicitly require a closing tag. For example, starting a new paragraph does not need a closing paragraph tag:

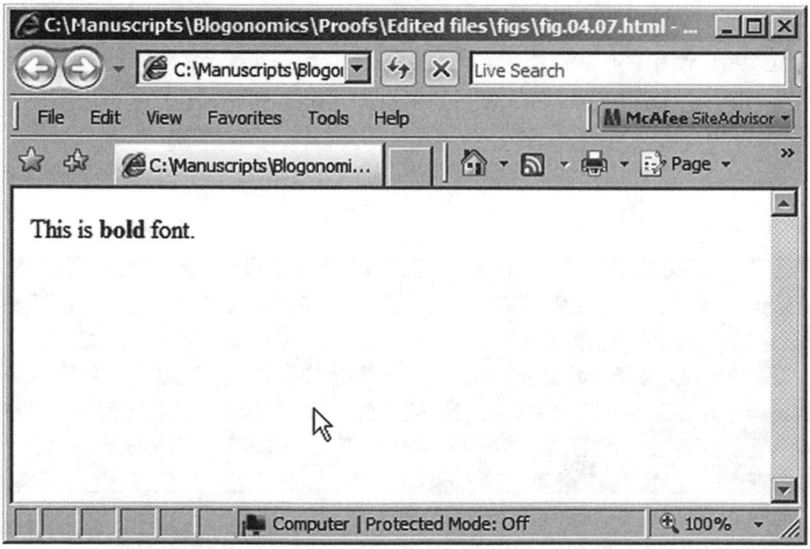

FIGURE 4.7: AN HTML FILE IS INTERPRETED BY YOUR BROWSER.

```
<P>This is a new paragraph.
```

- But you can add the closing paragraph tag:

```
<P>This is a new paragraph.</P>
```

- The only problem with not including a closing tag is that any visible change will not be undone until the closing tag is added. So the following expression will look like that shown in Figure 4.8, where all text after the opening <B> tag is bold font text, regardless of whether you want it all bold or not:

```
This is <B>bold font
```

- You can embed HTML opening and closing tags into a properly structured hierarchy (or proper nesting). So this is okay:

```
This is <B><I>bold italic</I></B> text.
```

- But you also don't have to embed HTML opening and closing tags into a properly structured hierarchy (i.e., you don't

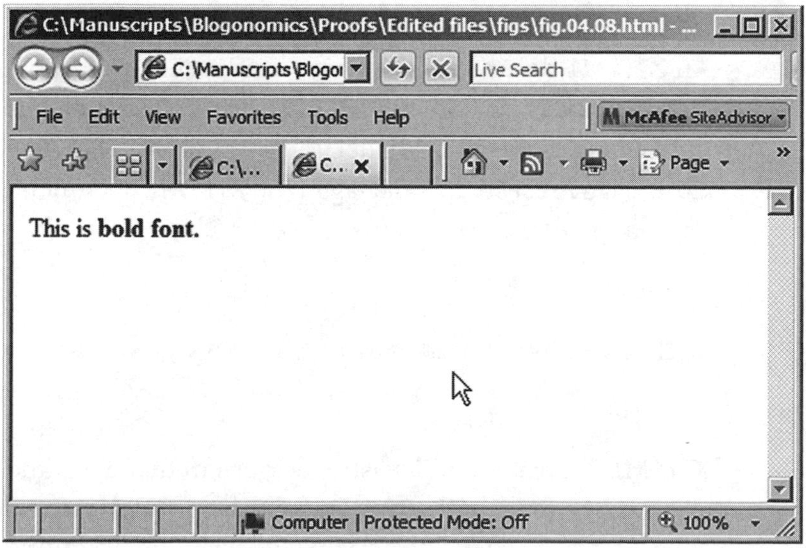

FIGURE 4.8: HTML DOES NOT REQUIRE CLOSING TAGS, BUT
SOMETIMES THEY ARE NEEDED.

have to nest opening and closing tags properly). So this is okay, too:

```
This is <B><I>bold italic</B></I> text.
```

- This is an empty tag in HMTL because there is no text between the tags:

```
<B></B>
```

- An empty element can also be displayed as <B/>.

- There is one final point to make about HTML, and it's probably the most important point—HTML has a fixed set of tags. You can't make up your own tags.

XHTML: HALF HTML AND HALF XML?

At this point, something called eXtensible Hypertext Markup Language (XHTML) comes into play. XHTML attempts to improve on HTML by adding some of the capacity of XML into HTML. The result is XHTML. XHTML has the following attributes, making XHTML documents what are known as *well-formed documents:*

- An XHTML document must have a single enclosing root tag called <HTML>. So the <HTML> opening tag must be the first tag in the XHTML document, and the </HTML> closing tag must be the final tag in the XHTML document. For example:

```
<HTML>

This is <B><I>bold italic</I></B> text.

</HTML>
```

- XHTML is cleaner and has stricter rules in that open and closing tags must both exist, and also be properly hierarchically structured (nested one inside the other according to the order that tags were opened).

- HTML tags are not case sensitive. XHTML tags must be all lowercase to prevent mismatched opening and closing tags simply because of case mismatches.

AND FINALLY TO XML

The eXtensible Markup Language (XML) is an extensible form of HTML. This means that XML allows creation of its own tags. Additionally, most of the restrictions of XHTML apply to XML, where hierarchical nesting structure must be strictly applied, and all open tags must have closing tags. Unlike XHTML however, XML tags are not required to be lowercase, but opening and closing tags must match exactly, including case sensitivity of all characters in an XML tag. In reality, HTML is intended only to display data visually in a browser. However, XML is intended to both display and describe data. As already stated, XML documents define and contain both data and metadata. HTML documents contain only data.

The advantage of XML is flexibility. XML can be used to create new markup languages (new vocabularies for different industries), because new tags can be created. This is what is really meant by the inclusion of Figure 4.6. This is the power of XML, which can be used to create a new programming language (for a browser), where that programming language allows for a specific application, industry, or topic to be explicitly catered to—of which RSS is no exception. RSS is written using XML and is intended to explicitly define feeds for broadcast over the Internet, changes to Web sites, blogs, podcasts, and so on.

One further aspect of XML is a special-purpose language called eXstensible Style Sheets (XSL). In its simplest form, XSL allows the application of consistent formatting of repetitive data structures across an XML document. The result is a template written in XSL, which is applied to duplicated data items in an XML document. For example, if you stored all your customer names and addresses in an XML document, you could display each customer's details in the same format, one after the other, where the same display rules (XSL template) are applied to each customer over and

over again. HTML also has its equivalent of XSL. The HTML equivalent is called Class Style Sheets (CSS). However, combining HTML
and CSS creates a slightly different version of HTML, which
is something else called Dynamic HTML (DHTML). DHTML
morphs into something that is not HTML. XSL, on the other hand,
makes no change to XML: XSL only further empowers XML.

Basic XML Syntax

We could proceed directly to RSS in order to explain XML. However, RSS is an application of XML, or a new extension and language on top of XML. So it might be better to explain XML from a
trivial perspective first and then to get to the definition of RSS documents. This is an example XML script containing a very small
number of stock exchange listings:

```
<?xml version="1.0"?>
<stocks>
   <exchange name"NYSE" location="New York">
      <index name="DOW" val="13,507.28"
      chg="+66.15" />
      <index name="NYSE Composite" val="9876.11"
      chg="+63.60" />
      <company ticker="IBM" name="International
      Business Machines">
         <price>$105.18</price>
         <change>+$1.23</change>
         <perc>+1.18%</perc>
      </company>
      <company ticker="BA" name="The Boeing
      Company">
         <price>$98.25</price>
         <change>+$0.83</change>
         <perc>+0.85%</perc>
      </company>
   </exchange>
   <exchange name="NASDAQ" location="New York">
      <index name="NASDAQ" val="2557.19"
      chg="+19.27" />
      <company ticker="ORCL" name="Oracle
```

```
      Corporation">
         <price>$19.24</price>
         <change>+$0.49</change>
         <perc>+2.61%</perc>
      </company>
   </exchange>
   <exchange name="FTSE" location="London">
      <index name="FTSE" val="6570.50" chg="+5.05"
      />
      <company ticker="BP" name="British
      Petroleum">
         <price>$567.500</price>
         <change>-$1.50</change>
         <perc>-0.26%</perc>
      </company>
   </exchange>
   <exchange name="CAC" location="Paris">
      <index name="CAC" val="6057,49" chg="+0,15"
      />
      <company ticker="DA" name="Dassault Systems">
         <price>$740.00</price>
         <change></change>
         <perc></perc>
      </company>
   </exchange>
   <exchange name="DAX" location="Frankfurt" />
</stocks>
```

The only absolutely required tag in an XML document is the first line, stating that it is an XML document and that your browser should parse (interpret) it as XML—and obviously not as HTML, Japanese, Martian, and anything else you can I can think of. Figure 4.9 shows how the preceding XML document looks when executed in your browser.

In Figure 4.9, we have closed the exchange tags (in the circle) for the New York Nasdaq, London, and Paris stock exchanges in order to fit the entire XML document into a more easily managed space for this graphical figure.

Now that you've seen what an XML document looks like, you

can examine the basic rules of XML—while looking at the XML document code you have just seen. The XML tag is mandatory and in its simplest form tells your browser which version of XML to use:

```
<?xml version="1.0"?>
```

One way of including a style sheet is by way of using the XSL tag:

```
<?xml:stylesheet type="text/xsl"href="stocks
.xsl"?>
```

Note: Every time a new data set is to be displayed on an HTML page, the HTML page must be rebuilt from scratch. You can use an XSL style sheet to apply a consistent template to repetitive data in an XML document, such as the repeated <exchange> elements shown in Figure 4.9. If exchange data is altered, you are updating only the XML document and not the XSL file as well. A similar result can be found by combining HTML and CSS into DHTML. However, XML and XSL are very much more powerful, versatile, and also much simpler than DHTML.

Every XML document has a single root node, embedding all content other than processing tags (<?xml ... >) between the opening and closing root node tags. In Figure 4.9, the root node is <stocks>, and closed with </stocks>. These are the general rules:

- All opening tags must have a closing tag:

```
<exchange> ... </exchange>
```

- An empty tag can be both an opening and closing tag:

```
<exchange />
```

- But this is still correct as an empty tag:

```
<exchange></exchange>
```

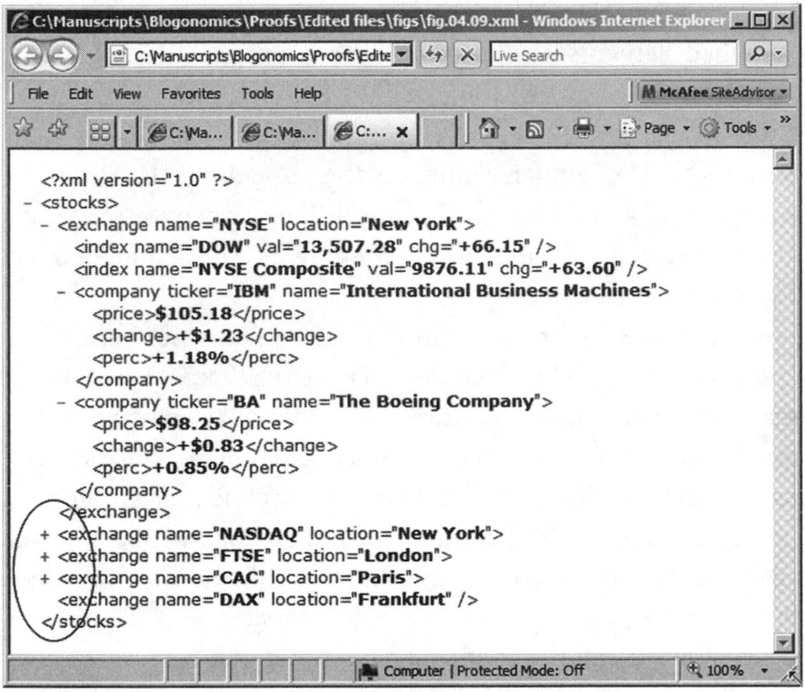

FIGURE 4.9: AN XML DOCUMENT RUNNING IN YOUR BROWSER.

- XML is case sensitive in that this is correct:

```
<Stocks> ... </Stocks>
```

- This is not correct and your browser will return an error:

```
<Stocks> ... </Stocks>
```

- XML requires proper hierarchically structured nesting. This is okay:

```
<stocks><exchange> ... </exchange></stocks>
```

- This is not okay:

```
<stocks><exchange> ... </stocks></exchange>
```

Those are the rules. There are some central pieces to XML, which are called elements, attributes, and namespaces.

Elements

So, an XML element (an element is the same thing as a tag) is the equivalent of an HTML tag. The only difference between XML and HTML elements is that in HTML they are limited and predefined. In XML you create the tags.

There are also very distinctly defined relationships between elements within an XML document. Those relationships as a whole make up a hierarchical structure, which looks like an upside-down tree. In short, every XML document has a root node. The root node has no parent nodes, it also has one or more child nodes, and it has no sibling nodes. At the bottom of the tree are the leaf nodes, which are leaves on the tree because they have no child nodes. In between the root node and all the leaves are the branch nodes. The branch nodes make up all the connections between the single root node and all the leaves. So an XML document like the one shown in Figure 4.9, if drawn out on a piece of paper looks something like that shown in Figure 4.10.

Attributes

Elements can also have attributes, which are essentially properties of each element rather than things contained within an element. In the following example, the name and location of the exchange are properties of the <exchange> element. A property therefore helps to describe or further specialize an element:

```
<exchange name="NYSE" location="New York">
```

There is often much debate over what should be stored as element or attribute. Some may argue that data should be stored in elements, and metadata should be stored as attributes. The downside to deploying metadata as attributes is that the metadata is no longer part of the hierarchical structure (the upside-down tree thing you see in Figure 4.10). The very heart of XML is that tree structure,

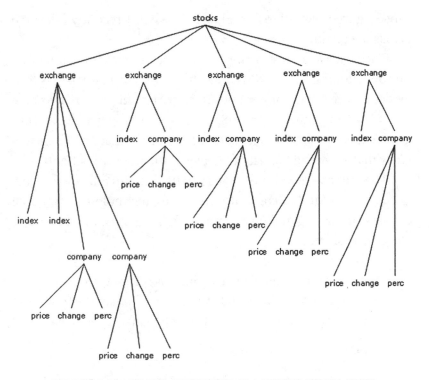

FIGURE 4.10: AN XML DOCUMENT IS A HIERARCHICAL TREE STRUCTURE.

which defines the relationships between different elements. Those relationships are metadata, in addition to the definitional type structure of attributes. Quite often, I find that metadata is slotted into attributes when one attempts to mimic a relational database structure into an XML document. This can be correct for some situations. However, XML document tree structure is in reality an object-style structure, which is completely contrary to that of relational database methodology. To find out more about relational database modeling, object modeling, and XML, you might like to read one of my other books (see *Beginning Database Design,* Powell-Gavin, Wrox, 2005, and *Beginning XML Databases,* Powell-Gavin, Wrox, 2006). And I'm sorry, but I don't have any freebies left because I gave them all to a local charity when I recently relocated across the country.

The best way to use attributes is not a technical one, but often one of flattening out the XML tree structure. The result is less text, less complexity, but longer lines in the script file. Also, if you are using XML to generate reporting from something like Access, Oracle Database, or SQL Server to a relational database, then it is likely that a flattened (attribute-heavy) structure is of better use.

The real power behind XML is in its flexibility to adapt to any need and any kind of computer modeling technology. Relational database modeling and object modeling are both computer modeling technologies.

Note: A computer modeling technology is simply a method of computerizing some kind of commercial operation from something else, such as a less efficient paper-based system.

The following is a section of the XML document previously displayed:

```
<?xml version="1.0"?>
<stocks>
   <exchange name"NYSE" location="New York">
     <index name="DOW" val="13,507.28"
     chg="+66.15" />
     <index name="NYSE Composite" val="9876.11"
     chg="+63.60" />
     <company ticker="IBM" name="International
     Business Machines">
        <price>$105.18</price>
        <change>+$1.23</change>
        <perc>+1.18%</perc>
     </company>
     <company ticker="BA" name="The Boeing
     Company">
        <price>$98.25</price>
        <change>+$0.83</change>
        <perc>+0.85%</perc>
```

```
    </company>
  </exchange>
  ...
```

The preceding example has much of its data embedded into elements as attributes. The attribute values can also removed as attributes and spread into the hierarchy, creating elements from the attributes, across the XML document as follows:

```
<?xml version="1.0"?>
<stocks>
  <exchange>
    <name>NYSE</name>
    <location>New York</location>
    <index>
      <name>DOW</name>
      <val>13,507.28</val>
      <chg>+66.15</chg>
    </index>
    <index>
      <name>NYSE Composite</name>
      <val>9876.11</val>
      <chg>+63.60</chg>
    </index>
    <company>
      <ticker>IBM</ticker>
      <name>International Business
      Machines</name>
      <price>$105.18</price>
      <change>+$1.23</change>
      <perc>+1.18%</perc>
    </company>
    <company>
      <ticker>BA</ticker>
      <name>The Boeing Company</name>
      <price>$98.25</price>
      <change>+$0.83</change>
      <perc>+0.85%</perc>
    </company>
  </exchange>
  ...
```

The preceding XML document sample essentially gives you a more visible picture of the structure of the data (what is contained within what, and how each element relates to other elements). Figure 4.11 shows the preceding attribute to element hierarchy, expanded example in graphical form—just for the sake of clarity.

The Importance of Namespaces

A namespace allows you to use a predefined language within XML, such as those shown in Figure 4.6. In other words, to use a specific definition such as Legal XML, allowing you to define legal documents as XML, or something like RSS for feeds—you point your XML document at a specific place on the Internet. The address on the Internet is a computer containing the definition of the XML

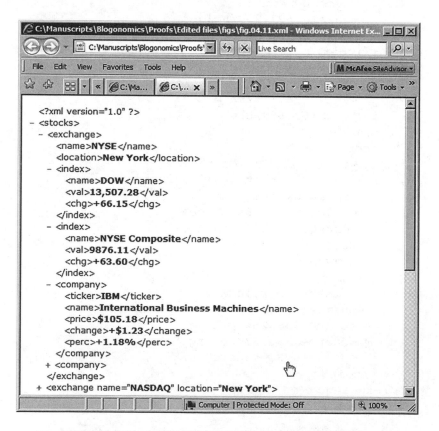

FIGURE 4.11: SPREADING ATTRIBUTES INTO ELEMENT HIERARCHICAL STRUCTURE.

you want to get at. In the case of the MySpace RSS document shown in Figure 4.5, the namespace used is a podcast broadcast from an iTunes Web site, which defines the format of the XML programming language coding for a version of RSS.

Additionally, a namespace allows you to store a definition. In terms of *How to Make Money with Your Blog,* you are interested in things like RSS and podcasts rather than Legal XML or Chemistry XML. This book is not about the law or mathematics.

A namespace is referred to at the beginning of an XML document. Any references for reinterpretation by the definition on a namespace Web site isf referred to in the XML document you are writing by pointing the XML element at the namespace, as shown in Figure 4.12.

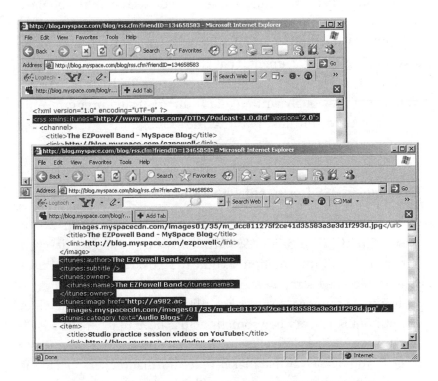

FIGURE 4.12: NAMESPACES ALLOW ACCESS TO SPECIFIC

INTERPRETATIONS.

The specific namespace definition shown in Figure 4.12 is the RSS namespace called iTunes. The iTunes namespace is accessed by the xmlns attribute, in the rss element, on the second line of the XML document, as shown in the top half of Figure 4.12. Specific element types defining various iTunes namespace and specific rss elements are shown in the lower half of Figure 4.12.

To reiterate, why are namespaces so important? A namespace allows a specific topic to be defined somewhere on the Internet. People like you, needing to write XML documents containing things like specialized mathematical formulas or something legal, for instance, can then import those definitions directly into your XML document. You don't have to know how something for a specific topic works—you just get to use it in XML. In other words, if you're looking for a specialized calculator, for example, you don't need to look up the formula, type it in, and execute it. All you need to do is access a namespace containing that calculator (such as Math XML) and then just go ahead and execute the formula on the data in your XML document. That's why namespaces are so important to XML—because namespaces allow individuals to take advantage of previously written and industry-tested programming language code. You just point to the code and use it. It makes things so much easier.

Building an RSS Document with XML

You should already have a fair idea of what RSS is. To recap, RSS is Really Simple Syndication. *Syndication* is a word used to describe broadcasting of information. Syndication over the Internet uses *feeds* (designated computers on the Internet), in order to automatically update changes to *subscribers* (those who request the feed) or to notify subscribers when something has been updated. RSS is effectively an XML dialect, allowing information fed by a specific site to be flavored in a way that makes that information personal to the perspective of the person accessing the feed.

When using RSS feeds, those feeds can be put together using a specific program or Web site called an *RSS aggregator*. The aggregator simply organizes and puts different feeds together for a user to get automated uploads. This way, people reading your blog don't have to go to your blog once a day to check for updates. Also, you don't have to spam them to keep reminding them. Most important, any changes you make are automatically broadcast to your subscribers. This means that they don't have to check regularly—most visitors will probably never check again unless reminded or unless they are stalking you. Then again, your blog is very well targeted and has lots of really useful information. Also, bloggers won't become disheartened with your blog when they check continuously and find nothing new. Instead they are informed automatically when you have something new to offer to repeat visitors. And you're not sending any spam, which can really irritate people!

> Note: RSS is commonly used on the Internet and can also be used with hand-held devices, including cell phones.

RSS SYNTAX

Now that you know what RSS is for, how do you go about creating an RSS document? First, there are a few versions. Use version 2. Many sites, including Blogger.com, use an older version (at the time of writing this book), but Blogger.com does actually allow a very slightly altered RSS feed, ramped up to version 2.

To create an RSS-formatted file, you must create a text file using a text editor like Windows Notepad. Also, an RSS text file is an XML file, so it's stored with an .xml extension.

Now you can read through the syntax elements of an RSS document.

An RSS Feed Is an Entire Blog . . . and a Channel

An RSS channel is the element in an RSS document defining the feed itself. It's like a sales channel where the channel passes from the producer of a product all the way through to a retailer. A product manufacturer makes a product. A distributor ships it out all over the place, delivering it to vendors and retailers. The sales channel is the path of companies and representatives a product takes to get all the way through to the customer. Similarly, an RSS feed feeds information to the Internet, which could be stuck together and organized by an aggregator or two, then passes it to your blog, and finally sends on to your customers. Your customer is a blogger reading your blog. In relation to a blog, the RSS channel represents your entire blog (all the postings and profile information on your blog).

An RSS sales channel has three obligatory elements with which it defines itself:

- <title>. This gives your feed a name. It has to have a name; otherwise nobody will know what it is, making them less likely to read it. And search engines will probably ignore you.

- <link>. This is the URL address of your channel. Without this, again, nobody will find your blog. For one of my blogs the link is as follows:

    `http://ezpowellmusic.blogspot.com`

    The preceding link is the DNS name address of one of my blogger addresses (URLs) on the Internet.

- <description>. This tells you what my blog is all about, which also encourages search engine scanning and other bloggers to read my blog.

So, my initial RSS document might look something like that shown in Figure 4.13.

In addition to the three mandatory <title>, <link>, and <description> elements, the <channel> allows a number of further contained elements with which to help in refining your blog:

- <category>. Aggregators will use this element to group your blog with similar blogs.

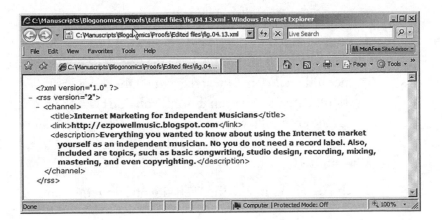

```
C:\Manuscripts\Blogonomics\Proofs\Edited files\fig.04.13.xml - Windows Internet Explorer

C:\Manuscripts\Blogonomics\Proofs\Edited files\fig.04.13.xml        Live Search

File   Edit   View   Favorites   Tools   Help                      McAfee SiteAdvisor

C:\Manuscripts\Blogonomics\Proofs\Edited files\fig.04...           Page    Tools

<?xml version="1.0" ?>
- <rss version="2">
  - <channel>
      <title>Internet Marketing for Independent Musicians</title>
      <link>http://ezpowellmusic.blogspot.com</link>
      <description>Everything you wanted to know about using the Internet to market
        yourself as an independent musician. No you do not need a record label. Also,
        included are topics, such as basic songwriting, studio design, recording, mixing,
        mastering, and even copyrighting.</description>
  </channel>
</rss>

Done                                    Computer | Protected Mode: Off        100%
```

FIGURE 4.13: A CHANNEL IS A FEED FOR YOUR BLOG.

- <copyright>. Applies a copyright notice into your content, always a good idea. Even if something is not specifically copyrighted, it scares people off from copying. Although you do want people to link to, or at least mention, your URL when they copy. Don't scare people too much; otherwise, nobody will take any notice of you.

Note: When your blog postings are uploaded on an initial date to a Web site like Blogger, that initial upload date cannot be changed. You can also create backups on read-only CD ROMs—file dates are written onto a fixed media storage such as CD-R. The dates can't be changed. You are copyright-protected because the initial creation date will determine who created it first. If you really concerned about copyright, you can always paper print entries with a date stamp on them.

- <image>. This option presents an image on the screen of a Blogger with your feed when displayed. Three elements are required to specifically define an image:

1. <url>. The Web site address location of your image.

2. <title>. Sets the ALT (HTML alternate) text for the image if the image is not found. This text also appears in a nice little yellow box on screen when the mouse is rolled over the image. So keep it brief. You don't want to block out the entire screen with an essay. I've done this before without realizing it and it can be a little awkward to explain.

3. <link>. Hyperlink to the Web site offering the channel.

- <language>. Aggregators obviously group blogs based on the language used. It makes sense to group all blogs written in Italian such that they are presented to Italian-speaking bloggers rather than Russian-speaking bloggers.

My RSS feed for my musicians' blog now looks like that shown in Figure 4.14.

Figure 4.15 shows a general listing of all mandatory and optional, child elements available to the RSS XML <channel> element.

An RSS Blog Posting Is an Item in a Channel

Postings are on your blog defined as <item> elements. Items are placed within a <channel> element. Each item also contains <title>, <link>, and <description> elements, as shown in Figure 4.16.

Figure 4.16 shows two of the postings defined for my Internet Marketing for Independent Musicians Blog on Google's Blogger.

Figure 4.17 shows a general listing of all mandatory and optional child elements as available to the RSS XML <item> element.

That's RSS syntax, which is written in XML. Now here's the interesting part. If you are using a simplistic blog platform, such as Google Blogger, and a feed aggregator like FeedBurner, then you don't need to know how to code RSS because these sites generate and manage all the RSS code for you. There are more complex

```
<?xml version="1.0" ?>
- <rss version="2">
  - <channel>
    <title>Internet Marketing for Independent Musicians</title>
    <link>http://ezpowellmusic.blogspot.com</link>
    <description>Everything you wanted to know about using the Internet to market yourself
      as an independent musician. No you do not need a record label. Also, included are
      topics, such as basic songwriting, studio design, recording, mixing, mastering, and even
      copyrighting.</description>
    <category>Songwriting</category>
    <copyright>© Gavin Powell 2006. All rights reserved.</copyright>
  - <image>

      <url>http://www.oracledbaexpert.com/graphics/AlbumCoverListenOnMySpace.jpg</url>
      <title>Bedroom Eyes, by The EZPowell Band</title>
      <link>http://www.oracledbaexpert.com</link>
    </image>
    <language>us-en</language>
  </channel>
</rss>
```

FIGURE 4.14: A <CHANNEL> CAN CONTAIN BOTH MANDATORY AND OPTIONAL ELEMENTS.

blog templates where you create the blog yourself, or use a template copied to your own server. In those more complex environments, you would have to code the RSS feed into an XML document yourself. Additionally, when writing programs and scripts such as XML documents, you have more direct control and

<channel> Child Elements	Mandatory	What does it do?
<category>		A feed can have one or more categories
<cloud>		Feed updates are instantly registered
<copyright>		Copyright notice
<description>	Yes	Channel (Blog) description
<docs>		Feed format documentation URL (Web site address)
<generator>		Generate the feed with a specific tool or program
<image>		Displays an image when an aggregator presents your feed to Bloggers
<language>		Language specification such as us-en for American-English
<lastBuildDate>		Last modification date of your Blog
<link>	Yes	Internet URL to your Blog
<managingEditor>		Editor's email address
<pubDate>		Most recent published date of your Blog
<rating>		Internet PICS (Platform for Internet Content Selection) rating
<skipDays>		Days specified for aggregators to skip feed updates
<skipHours>		Hours specified for aggregators to skip feed updates
<textInput>		Display a text input field on Blogger's screen with the feed display
<title>	Yes	The name of your Blog (channel)
<ttl>		Minutes between browser refreshes
<webMaster>		Webmaster's email address

FIGURE 4.15: RSS XML <CHANNEL> CHILD ELEMENTS.

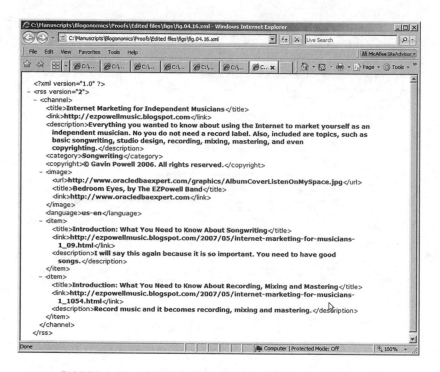

FIGURE 4.16: A BLOG (CHANNEL) CONTAINS ONE OR MORE ITEMS (BLOG POSTINGS).

access to all possible RSS elements and settings. But it is a lot more difficult. If you want to focus on the task of blogging, you will probably want to start your first blog and feed with Google Blogger and FeedBurner.

\<item\> Child Elements	Mandatory	What does it do?
\<author\>		Author's email address
\<category\>		An item can have one or more categories
\<comments\>		Links to commetary
\<description\>	Yes	Item (posting) description
\<enclosure\>		Adds a media file to the item
\<guid\>		Uniquely identifies an item
\<link\>	Yes	Sets a URL for the item
\<pubDate\>		Most recent publication, or re-edition date
\<source\>		A third-party source of somethin copied or duplciated, with permission of course
\<title\>	Yes	Names the item

FIGURE 4.17: RSS XML \<ITEM\> CHILD ELEMENTS.

Publishing a Feed without RSS

When you blog using MySpace Blogging or Google Blogger, and even when you publish a feed using FeedBurner, it's all interactive and there are lots of choices. Blogger and FeedBurner generate all the required RSS code for you. All the coding becomes transparent.

> Note: The word *transparent* is computer industry jargon for "you don't have to think about it!" You don't have to worry about it and you don't have to program it—which is really great.

Transparency means you can get on with what your real reason for blogging: to generate advertising revenue—not to be hassled and slowed by technical details.

Two screens on Blogger, as shown in Figure 4.18, are all you need to set in order to configure your Google Blogger—to syndicate your blog as a feed to the Internet at large.

Now you get to go to a Web site called FeedBurner, which is located at www.feedburner.com. As of the time of writing this book,

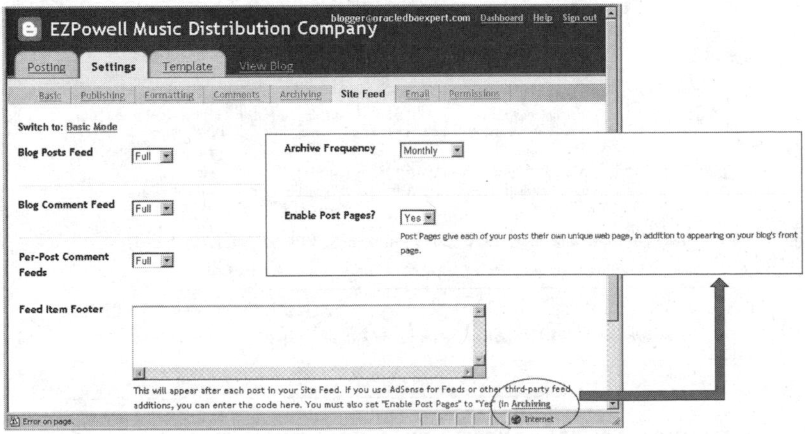

FIGURE 4.18: SETTING UP A FEED FROM GOOGLE BLOGGER.

FeedBurner incorporates a bunch of help button links right in the center of its main screen, as highlighted by the ellipse shown in Figure 4.19.

To use FeedBurner, you have to register first. As soon as I register a new username on FeedBurner, I get a screen as shown in Figure 4.20. At this point I type in the Internet address (URL or DNS name) of my blog, which is this:

```
ezpowellmusic.blogspot.com
```

In Figure 4.21, you can see for yourself that Google's Blogger has created RSS documents for my blog in both older and more up-to-date forms of RSS. Blogger doesn't even think it necessary to show me the RSS code—the detail is not necessary for me to create and set up my feed. Blogger does all the RSS coding for you—you don't have to write any RSS code if you don't want to.

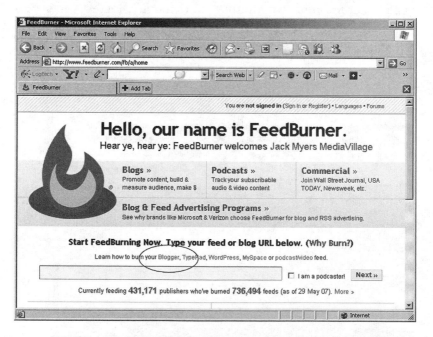

FIGURE 4.19: FEEDBURNER EVEN TELLS YOU HOW TO SET UP
WITH COMMON BLOG PLATFORMS.

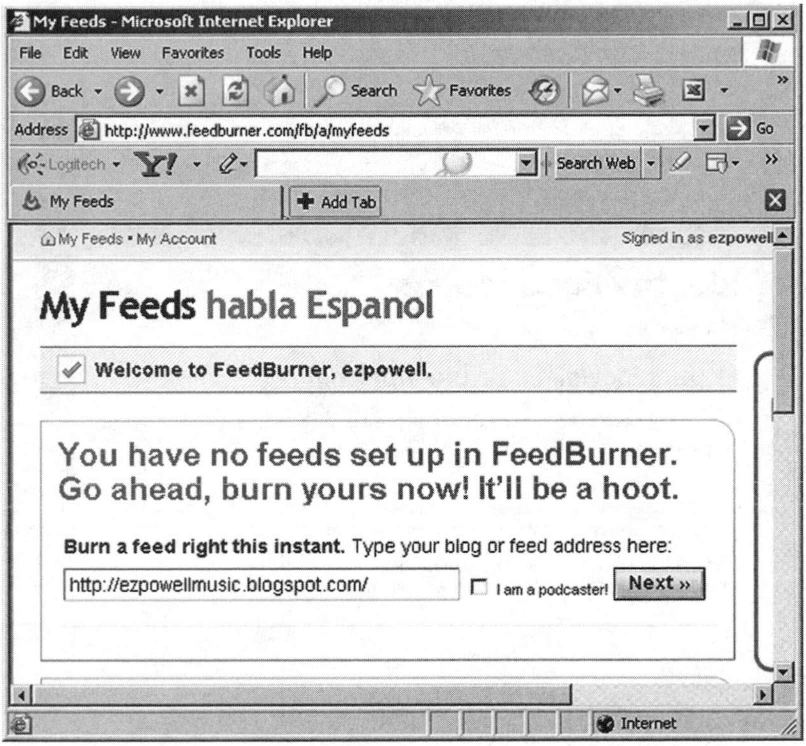

FIGURE 4.20: PUBLISHING A FEED ON FEEDBURNER IS AS EASY AS ABC.

The only thing I have changed in Figure 4.21, is that I have selected RSS 2 rather than RSS 1. The next thing to be done is to give your feed a name, as shown in Figure 4.22. The name of my blog (my blook) is "Internet Marketing for Independent Musicians by EZPowell."

Note: A *blook* is a book written as a blog.

Note: If you really want to get into the details of coding your blog, you can use a Web site at www.feedpublish.com to manage your RSS feed publishing activities.

FIGURE 4.21: BLOGGER HAS CREATED RSS CODE THAT
FEEDBURNER FINDS WITH EASE.

The next few screens following the screen shown in Figure 4.22 tell me that my feed is activated and that they would like to offer me further services, for a fee. In the tradition of the Internet, I find that there is usually a way to get something done for free, so I opt not to pay any money and stick to the free side of FeedBurner for now.

The next screen that is really interesting is the one shown in Figure 4.23. It says that I can automatically set up feeds for both Blogger and MySpace.

Looking at Figure 4.23, I have a blog on both Blogger and MySpace. I will be publishing a chicklet (a small graphic that looks like

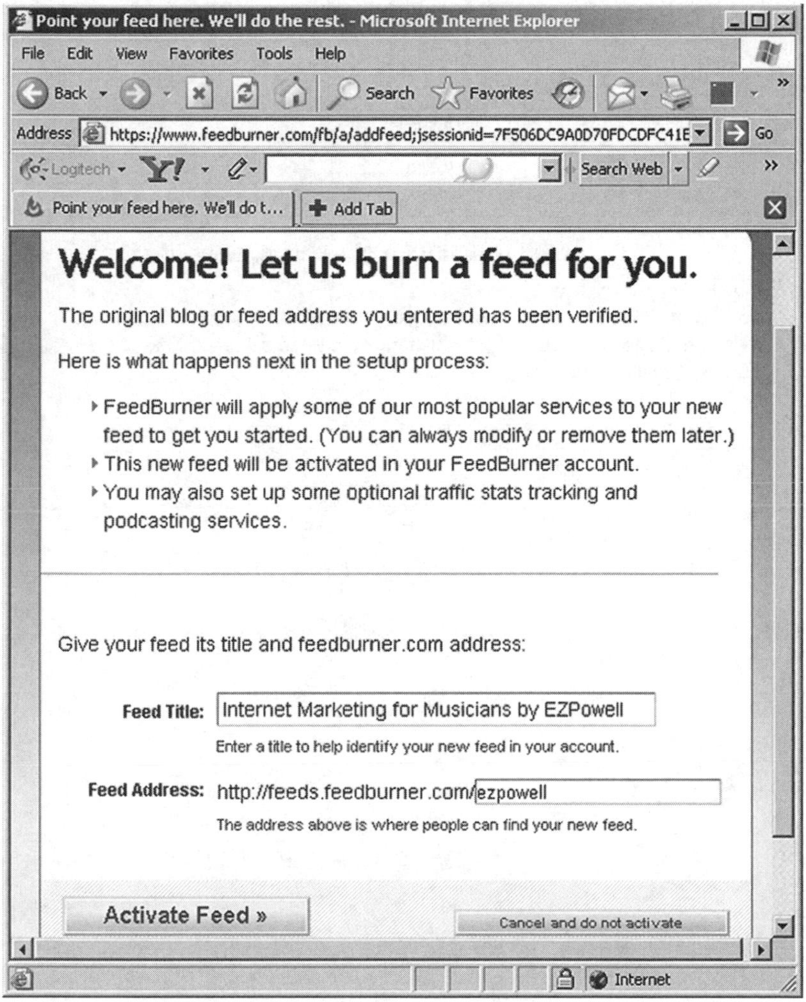

FIGURE 4.22: GIVE YOUR FEED A NAME.

blog reader), and I will be offering blog updates via email—for both my Blogger and my MySpace blogs. What you do at this stage is your choice, but if you wish to do the same, simply follow the instructions on the screen for FeedBurner. You have already seen how easy all thus stuff is—there is no need for further details in this book.

After I set everything up on all my blogs and Web sites, I get

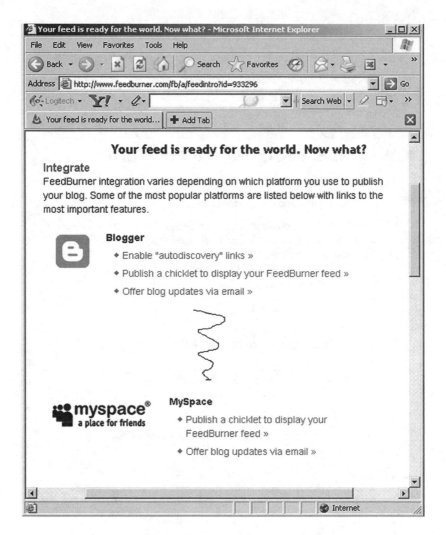

FIGURE 4.23: FEEDBURNER ALLOWS AUTOMATED FEED SETUP.

the results highlighted in the ellipses shown in Figures 4.24, 4.25, and 4.26.

Reading a Feed

Once again, when reading a feed, you can go through the entire gamut of setting up your RSS files, setting up your own feed, and

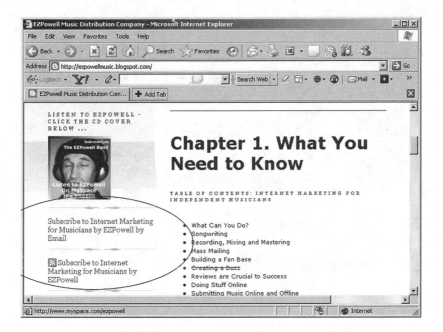

FIGURE 4.24: SETTING FEEDS UP ON BLOGGER.

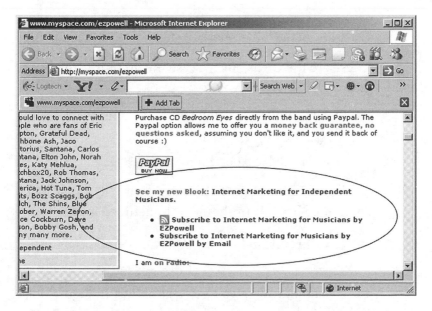

FIGURE 4.25: SETTING UP FEEDS ON MYSPACE.

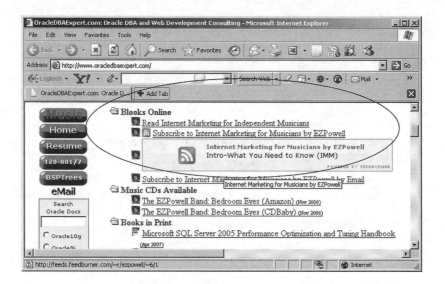

FIGURE 4.26: SETTING UP FEEDS ON AN INDEPENDENT WEB SITE.

setting up your own feed reader. But guess what? You can also do it the easy way:

- Go to any of the URLs shown in Figures 4.24, 4.25, or 4.26.

- These are the URLs, just in case the graphics are not too clear:

    ezpowellmusic.blogspot.com

    myspace.com/ezpowell

    www.oracledbaexpert.com

- Find the link on any of the preceding URLs that looks something like this (it should be underlined in blue):

    Subscribe to Internet Marketing for Musicians by EZ Powell

- Click that link. What you get is as shown in Figure 4.27. You can make your own choice at this point about how you

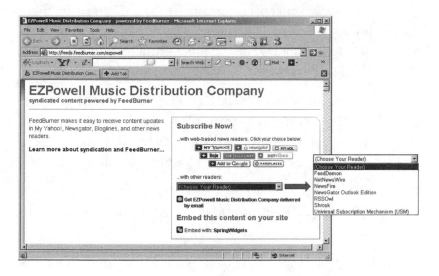

FIGURE 4.27: SETTING UP A FEED READER.

set up your feed. I could also include all the feed options as buttons, giving my blog readers the variety of choice—but that might make my blog pages look a little too cluttered and perhaps unappealing.

SUMMARY

Blogging really does simplify online publishing, and it may even someday fully replace book publishing. As coauthor of this book, I am currently attempting to write a book in a blog. It's called a *blook*.

You have to complete a number of simple tasks regularly to keep your blog focused, productive, and under control. Keep the following tasks in mind:

- *Spam.* Control spam comments on your blog. There is nothing that puts people off faster than junk.

- *Freebies.* Internet users just dig freebies. Then again, there is a lot of free stuff out there, so be sure to offer something of value without wasting people's time. Your time is valuable and so is theirs.

- *How to Make Money with Your Blog.* It's a business. It can be. The first step is to treat it like a business. This doesn't mean you pick things you don't like, but keep your goals in mind, and take little steps at a time. Reading this book helps!

- *Spreading the word.* Spread the word of your new Blog with feeds.

At this stage, you might have gone ahead and begun the process of creating a blog for yourself. You had the germ of an idea and created a blog using something like Google's Blogger. With this chapter, you can attempt to persuade a few more people to notice you. So, maybe go and create a simple feed for your blog on FeedBurner.

There's no time like the present.

EXTRAS AND **INSPIRATION**

WHAT'S IN THIS CHAPTER?

This chapter ties up a few loose ends that can't be left out but that wouldn't fit too well elsewhere. Blogging is all about communication. That communication is all typed on a computer keyboard, but the basic principle of winning friends and influencing people still applies.

Note: The communication aspect of blogging using a computer keyboard may well

change sometime in the future to include audio and video.
Computer technology changes very fast. The words audioblogging and videoblogging are already being used as
computer and blogging jargon. There is even a Web site
called www.audioBlog.com.

This chapter also gives you some general comments and advice on how to be successful as a blogger and how to tap into the
power and reach of leading blogs and blogging platforms such as
MySpace.

BLOG COMMUNICATIONS SKILLS

Blogging has a language and culture all of its own. It's essential
that you realize that being a good communicator when blogging is
no different than in any other medium. Proper grammar and language skills are essential. This means using proper punctuation
and following the basic rules of language—whichever language
you're writing in. Communicating via a blog entails all these
things, along with a serious commitment to honesty and transparency and a firm grasp on your own views on a topic. Take your
time when writing, as your collection of posts will build a picture
of your individual style for your readers—some will like it, others
won't.

Know Your Audience

One of the most important things to remember is your target audience. To whom are you trying to blog—and why? In short, you
need to know your audience. Lonely hearts who are using MySpace
or Friendster to try to find a date are unlikely to be particularly interested in a blog about Jeeps or Harry Potter books. Similarly,

Harry Potter fans might not be too keen on heavy metal music with lots of noisy, distorted electric guitars. Well they might like loud, ear-ringing, heavy metal music in addition to Harry Potter books, but you are more likely to spark some interest by focusing on one or the other, not both. Focus on a target audience that will produce the results you want. Random scanning of wide Internet populations has much lower response rates than a targeted appeal. Sure, crossover topics of heavy metal music and Harry Potter are possibilities. However, it is better to try to get at Harry Potter fans when trying to talk about Harry Potter books. And focus on heavy metal music fans when you are trying to promote a heavy metal music band. Don't you agree?

You have to target your audience and market to a group of people who will return the best value and result for your efforts. Gavin has experimented with Web sites for years, including MySpace and YouTube. Randomly picking people from a list of general users on a social network Web site generally attracts very little response. On the contrary, let's say you are looking to attract fans who like JJ Cale music because you have found an indie musician who sounds very much like JJ Cale. Go to JJ Cale's MySpace and YouTube profiles and spend some time chatting up his fans. You might net far more people who will actually buy the indie musician's latest CD.

So, targeting your audience is all about aiming at people who are most likely to respond. And, obviously, you have to know who those people might be. You have to know your audience. You have to have a good idea of who you want to market to and thus what those people might be interested in. The goal of advertising is to get someone to take an action—like making a purchase. That can be something sold by you or by someone else paying you to advertise for them.

Blogging is nothing without readers. Those readers will be disappointed if what they read in your blog is not what they expect, or if it's about something they are not interested in. Disappointed readers will go elsewhere. Interested readers will come back for more. The more you know about your audience, the more likely you are to attract a larger and more positive response. So, the more you know about your topic, the more likely you are to create useful, relevant content . . . which will lead to pleased readers who not only come back, but who will tell others about your blog. The more you know about your readers, the more you can create content they will like.

Surviving the Blogosphere

Surviving the blogosphere can be like learning a new language. Internet phrases and acronyms such as LOL have been around for years. Well perhaps they have been around for 10 years. In the world of computers, including the Internet and blogging, things change very, very fast—often on a weekly basis. It's difficult for even a computer- and Internet-savvy person to keep up with all of the changes. Sometimes it's like living in a blur. Have you ever been to a racetrack and taken a still photograph of a race car at exactly the moment it screams past you? When you develop your picture, it's just a blur of color, which can be fun—but indiscernible if you didn't take the picture. Changes in the online world can come up that fast . . . and they never stop. As soon as one change becomes accepted en masse as the new norm, other change appears. So you need to be on your toes and develop a system for keeping up with the changes that matter to you or that affect your topic of interest.

Part of surviving the blogosphere and being a blogger is talking the same language that everyone else does. Also, much of this blogspeak stuff is used in instant messenger tools.

> Note: An instant messenger is a tool used to send messages back and forth between two people over the Internet in real time . . . a little like a telephone call, only in text form on a computer screen.

Instant messenger tools allow for instant communication. In some respects blogspeak and Internet acronyms have evolved from the need to type faster in real time. Typing "LOL" on a keyboard is much easier than punching in "laughing out loud," one letter at a time, as many hunt-and-peck artists are destined to do.

Blogspeak: The Language of Blogging

The language of blogging is essentially the same language as is used for countless Internet tools and activities, including e-mail, instant messaging, and blogging. There are some language alterations that are specific to blogging, but it's all the language of the Internet. Many of the acronyms used resulted from the need to type things quickly. There are also things called *emoticons,* which allow you to express simple emotions, such as a smile, a maniacal laugh, or a frown. In some tools, emoticons are used to express more complex emotions. Emoticons are becoming part of the language of blogging. Many blog platforms, such as WordPress, automatically recognize the combination of certain characters and insert the related emoticon image into the spot where the characters appear in your typing. So, in a platform like WordPress, typing a colon and a closing parenthesis together, :), converts to a little smiley face when you publish the post live to the Internet.

The point is that the Internet is altering language and inventing an expressive shorthand all its own, driven by the people who use that language, so it's popular and also very practical. One of the oddest things for any new blogger or Internet user is to be confronted with something such as "LOL" or "FWIW" (for what it's worth). This language is constantly evolving and changing, so you're bound to encounter something new to you almost weekly. If you find something new and want to try it out, you'd best make sure it means what you think it means. Nothing looks worse than a blog post with the wrong use of an acronym when the writer is trying to be witty. To keep up to speed on the latest additions to the "acronym language," just stick that phrase into your favorite search engine and see what comes back.

To survive the blogosphere, it helps to know your audience and to have some idea of the lingo of the Internet. You should invest some time and develop a working knowledge of blogspeak acronyms, words, and phrases. At the very least, learning to be proficient in communicating in this manner will inject some personality into your blog.

Here are some terms and their basic meanings. Others may define them slightly differently, but this is how we define them:

- *Snark.* This is a blog, posting, or blogger who is nasty and obnoxious. Words like *hater* in the urban dictionary (see www.urbandictionary.com) apply in this case, perhaps. There are also some less pleasant words used to describe a snark.

- *Macrologue.* Microcosmic is small scale. Macrocosmic is large scale. In the world of blogging, a macrologue is a little like a conversation going on between lots of people, on a global scale, on many blogs all at the same time. In other words, a really big conversation.

- *Moblog.* A blog is a Web log typed into a computer and stored in a database on a server computer somewhere. A moblog is simply a blog entered into a computer system using some kind of mobile device. In other words, a moblog is a mobile blog.

- *Kudos.* This is a word that has been around for a few hundred years. It is commonly used on MySpace blog postings to allow blog readers to send praise to the blogger who typed in the original posting.

- *Megablog.* This blogging word is used to describe a really big, very busy blog.

There is a lot more to blogspeak and the language of blogging than what has been briefly mentioned here. The goal of this book is to help you figure out how to make money with your blog, not to teach you a new language. The easiest way to find out more about blogging and blogspeak is to search the Internet yourself. Again, you can easily go to a search engine such as Google, Yahoo, or

MSN/Live and look for a single word or an acronym that you are not sure of. Or you can search for a blogging dictionary to find a list of terms. There are some decent blogging dictionaries out there:

- David Gagne: www.davidgagne.net/index.php?p=3958

- The Giant Blogging Terms Glossary: www.quickonlinetips .com/archives/2006/06/the-giant-Blogging-terms-glossary

- Blog Terms Glossary: http://whatis.techtarget.com/ definition/0,289893,sid9_gci1186975,00.html

If you really want to impress coworkers, friends, and youngsters, you can start with this list of helpful and fun-to-use acronyms:

HTH	Hope this helps
IMHO	In my humble opinion
IMO	In my opinion
TTFN	Ta ta for now
ROFL	Rolling on the floor laughing
LOL	Laugh out loud
FWIW	For what it's worth
AFAIK	As far as I know
L8er	Later

These are some common acronyms and terms used in online and search marketing:

ATW/AllTheWeb	AllTheWeb.com: A search engine using fast technology hosting its own database
AV/AltaVista	AltaVista.com: A search engine hosting its own database
Bobby	Web accessibility standards and validation

CLICK-THRU	A click on an ad (the user clicks through to the advertised site)
CPA	Cost per acquisition
CPC	Cost per click
CPM	Cost per mil (per 1,000 impressions)
CTR	Click-through rate
DMOZ	Open Directory Project, DMOZ.org, a volunteer-based Web directory
Google	Google.com: A search engine hosting its own database
IE	Internet Explorer Web browser
IMPRESSION	Displaying an ad
Konqueror	Linux-based Web browser
Lead	Potential client generated via marketing initiatives
Link bait	Well-written, unique content designed to attract links
LookSmart	Looksmart.com: A PPC-type directory hosting its own database
Mozilla/Firefox	Open-source Web browser project that was the basis for Netscape Navigator
Metatags	Common name applied to the title, description, and keyword tags found in a page's code
NN	Netscape Navigator Web browser
ODP	Open Directory Project, DMOZ.org, a volunteer-based Web directory

Opera	Opera Web browser
PFI	Pay for inclusion
PFP	Pay for performance
PPC	Pay per click, the act of paying for placement on a per-click basis. Similar to Google's AdWords and Yahoo's Overture
PR	PageRank: Google-determined value of Your Web page
ROI	Return on investment
RON	Run of network
ROS	Run of site
SEM	Search engine marketing
SEO	Search engine optimization or optimizer
SERP	Search engine results page
Spam	Any unethical technique used by an SEO to gain better search engine ranking
TBPR	ToolBar PageRank: A visible approximation of your PageRank as shown via the Google ToolBar
w3c/w3c.org	World Wide Web Consortium, w3c.org, determines and posts Web standards for page creation

The following are helpful resources:

www.netlingo.com/inframes.cfm

www.cadenza.org/search_engine_terms/srchad.htm (an excellent glossary)

THE BLOGOSPHERE

What is the blogosphere? You can only assume that it is the Internet equivalent of biosphere or atmosphere. In the world of science, biosphere is a term used to encompass the part of the earth and its surrounding atmosphere that contains all life on planet Earth. The *atmosphere* is the gaseous part above the earth's surface, regardless of whether there is anything alive in it or not. The blogosphere is that part of the Internet containing blogs, the activity of blogging, and the presence of living biochemical creatures known as bloggers. So far, all bloggers are probably biochemical, but there may come a time when creativity becomes a part of artificial intelligence. Just imagine that! The blogging equivalent of a syndicated column in the New York Times or the London Standard, written by a blogging computer. How bizarre you might say. In this world, anything is possible.

BLOG CULTURE

What is blog culture? Now that's an interesting one. Traditionally, the Internet has been a place of free expression, free speech, free trade, and just about everything else. Blogging has essentially become just another extension. Governments and some corporate giants, even in this democratic republic, have on numerous occasions sought to throttle that freedom of expression. Fortunately, for the world as a whole, the political powers that be and the corporate magnates have so far not succeeded in stifling freedom of expression on the Internet or in taxing its use. So far, so good!

Blog culture is essentially an extension of Internet culture—that of freedom of expression. Obviously one blogger's right to freedom of expression gives another the right to either ignore you or insult you—that's life. Of course, from a negative perspective, blogging gives anyone and everyone with a gripe a fair voice. There are a billion Internet users. There are fewer bloggers, of course, so there are plenty of gripes—many of which are likely to be simply ignored. Blogging is a free form communication medium. If you don't like someone's opinions, then you don't have to read them.

BLOG ETIQUETTE

Is there a certain etiquette to follow when blogging? There certainly is. Etiquette is really a set of unwritten rules. It's a little like playing the game of golf, where every rule does have a sensible reason for its existence. For example, stand perpendicular to the line of the swinging driver when the current player is driving a golf ball off the tee. That's the point when a golfer (or, in my case, hacker) hits the ball as hard as possible all the way down the fairway. Given my handicap of about 901, standing perpendicular to my swing means that you are less likely to get clobbered with a seriously sliced golf ball—but it's not impossible. Why? Well I have managed a 90-degree slice at a driving range—once. I got some very dirty looks on that occasion. I have since given up the game of golf because I considered myself a danger to those around me. But that's the reason you stand perpendicular to the swinging club when a golfer hits that little white ball. Standing in front of a golfer who is teeing off is not very bright. That's the reason for one odd little rule of the game of golf.

Similarly, another rule of etiquette for the game of golf is not shouting out someone's name or making other loud noises as a golfer attempts a crucial putt. It's simply not done. It's very unfair, as it could put the other player off. It's just not very sporting. That's another unwritten rule, and thus considered etiquette, which is more of an acceptable practice rather than a punishable offence.

Blogging etiquette is more about being honest, not referring people to unpleasant Web sites, and being aware that whatever you are publishing (yes, I said *publishing*) will be with you for the rest of your life! Remember that one. Spell-check, because some people cannot spell, and frequent typos and spelling errors can make for an awkward read. After all, you want people to come back, don't you? Above all, speak for yourself, perhaps even about yourself, and don't misrepresent others—because, as with talking during another golfer's putt, it's unfair.

BLOGGING SUCCESS AND HOW TO GET IT

What makes a blog a success story? Good question. And are there any million-dollar bloggers? Yes. There are a few. However, let's make one thing clear. If you're in it for the dough, and just for the dough, it is unlikely you will have the determination to keep at it. In short, to make money from blogging, it's probably going to take you a long, long time. Not days or weeks, but probably months and maybe even years. It's all about building a name for yourself. It's brand building. Think about how long it took a product such as Tide (laundry detergent). How long did it take to build the Tide brand name? When I'm pushing a cart down the aisle in my local supermarket, am I more likely to grab the Tide and chuck it into the shopping cart? Yes, much more likely. Part of the reason for my lack of browsing is because I'm always shopping in a hurry. I find shopping completely uninteresting. I have heard of Tide. I've seen it on TV and here and there and everywhere. It's a brand. Subconsciously, my brain just tells me "uh-huh." And I grab the Tide. That is what brand building is.

Do that with your blog, and all the riches of the world could be yours. Procter & Gamble, the company that manufactures Tide, spends millions of dollars a year on advertising. That's how difficult and expensive brand building is. Advertisers want to etch the name of a product into your subconscious. Sounds a bit subversive, doesn't it? Well, it is, but it's psychological, and that's what branding is all about—owning a piece of real estate in *your* mind.

So, do you have a chance of succeeding as a blogger? Yes, but only with persistence. There is no one secret to success, but there are some general guidelines. Blogonomically speaking, you want to make some revenue. So stay focused on the bottom-line goals to make that happen. In the meantime, here are some points to consider that will help you plan your way to success.

- *How long until revenue?* This is the big one. Pick the right niche, write well, cover the basic marketing opportunities available to you, and you could see revenue in a matter of days or weeks. Not huge amounts, but you have to have pennies to save dollars. If you take your time when planning your work and then work that plan—have faith in your plan and watch you stats daily—soon enough you'll see dollars piling up.

- *Writing skills.* Successful bloggers have consistently good writing skills. It might seem far-fetched, but if you find your own writing skills lacking, yet you have the know-how and expertise in your field, you could always decide to team up with someone who writes well.

- *Interesting content.* Content has to be interesting. Readers may well be interested in your subject matter, but if it's not interesting, they will go elsewhere. If your content is really boring, they might say nasty things about your blog. How can content be made interesting? Here's an example. Gavin tried running a political blog. He received no comments but was building readership. He attempted to garner interest by being deliberately controversial. However, Blogger (the platform he used) has a little button on it where people can mark something as having offensive content. Essentially, the blog was shut down for having offensive content, which of course simply meant that a lot of people didn't agree with his postings/opinions. It proved the point he was exploring: anything controversial and generally objectionable will attract readership, but not necessarily the kind that you want. If someone reacts negatively to your blog, then they are unlikely to do you the favor of clicking on your ads. It's not about depth or attracting attention, or even evoking emotional responses (positive ones can help). It's more about getting and keeping people's attention. We can't tell you how to do this, because it's indescribable and unquantifiable. Try surfing the channels on your TV. What catches your interest? What do you watch for more than seven seconds? Think about those TV shows. What do they have that is compelling, interesting, engaging—even addictive? There is *something* there. Figure it out. Then try to apply it to your blog. It's less about how many articles you post, how long they are, whether or not you can spell, or what you write about—and more about making it fun and interesting.

- *Niche marketing.* Niche markets appear to be more likely to meet with success, but some wide-audience blogs have success as well. However, those wide-audience blogs are often run by people who understand blogging very well and who have been successful bloggers for a long time. For example, experienced bloggers will often spend money on advertising their blogs as a brand-building exercise. As an amateur, you might want to stick to a niche. But then again, if you can afford to throw money at advertising, then why not? Just make sure the subject matter of your blog will appeal to your target audience. You could always test the waters first, before laying out your hard-earned cash. Truly, though, the biggest bang for your efforts is in targeting the right niche and building a name for yourself within it. Do this well and you will be a go-to resource on the subject, an actual authority, with the readership and revenues to move in new directions if you choose.

- *Comments.* Make use of commentary mechanisms. Encourage bloggers to take part in your blog. You want your readers to make comments. And even add your own comments as replies to their comments, showing readers that you are immersed in your blog and that your readers' opinions count. Their opinions and expertise are important to you—make that clear by being interactive rather than just posting and walking away. Much of blogging is about communication. Communicate! Any commentary you can get from famous or well-known people will help—and could even help a lot. Specific MySpace commentary from one or two rock stars has helped Gavin to attract more attention than any other single thing. Be careful when approaching celebrities, though, for there's a very fine line between praise and stalking. And you can always just ask for help directly from someone with a good reputation. If that person likes what you blog about, there is no reason why he or she should object. Remember that famous people read blogs, too. And rock stars on MySpace listen to indie music as well.

- *Topical.* If your blog is topical, such as politics, then make sure it's current. By the way, as topics, politics and UFOs will not attract blogging advertising revenue. Regardless of the topic you choose, stay on topic. Do not start to wander into new areas, as your readers may simply decide to not follow. If you have another great idea for a blog, start a new blog on the topic—do not dilute the focus of a current blog by trying to make it reach in too many directions at the same time.

- *Updating your blog daily.* The more active you are, the better. Brief daily updates are better than one posting per week, or even seven postings over the weekend. At the very least, be consistent. Three to five postings of about 200 or so words each should be fine. Keep each unique. See, we told you it would take time.

- *Ad styles versus download speed.* Be careful when placing ads on your blog. Text ads tend to perform better than most image-based ads. All-text ads also load more quickly for users, thus speeding the loading of the entire page and improving their experience. Excessive heavy bandwidth content (videos, heavily animated ads) can take too long to download, sometimes even on a high-speed Internet connection. Speed is critical, because you can lose people before they even start reading. Musicians on MySpace and YouTube, who flood their profiles with interactive media sometimes have the lowest hit rates of all. Nobody can load their Web pages.

Look to the most popular blogs of the day for advice about how they are succeeding. After reading this book, go to the Internet and search Google or Yahoo for terms such as "top blogs," "success blogs," and so on. See what you can find. The computer industry traditionally changes very, very fast. The Internet is the same. As a blogger, use all the tools at your fingertips, and search for information on the Internet. But don't believe everything you read. For example, when searching on Google, the first items appearing on the search engine results page (SERP) are often paid ads from Google. They appear first, just above the very top of the list of results. These items are there to sell products, so unless you're looking to buy something, skip them and stick with the organic listings on the main portion of the page—those results will contain what you want. Look at Figure 5.1.

In Figure 5.1, the circled parts are sponsored search results. In other words, they have been paid for. These paid-for search engine ads sometimes provide useful information, but remember, advertisers pay to get their sites listed at the top. For example, examine the link at the top right under Sponsored Links. Typically, Gavin would search a term such as "Oracle expert" to find Web sites where he could get *free* information on Oracle Database. (When you are simply researching, why pay for information? The Internet is overflowing with it!) The top-right link is an ad placed by an online job-listing site, telling where to find Oracle Database experts for hire. Obviously, if Gavin were a manager searching for an em-

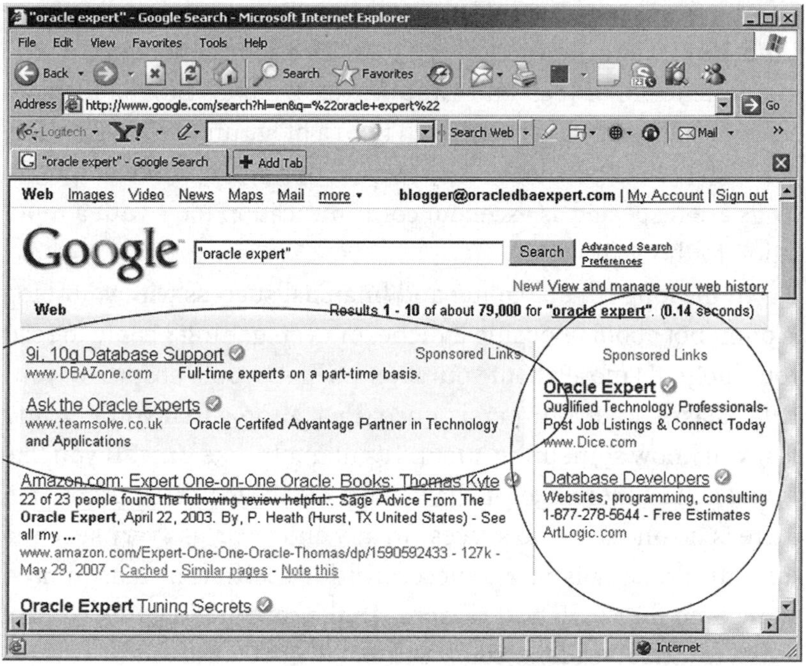

FIGURE 5.1: THE CIRCLED ITEMS ARE ADS THAT ADVERTISERS PAY GOOGLE TO SHOW IN THOSE SPOTS. WHILE USEFUL FOR SHOPPING, THEY ARE MUCH LESS SO FOR RESEARCHING.

ployee, this would be useful. In his case, he was looking for interesting blogs to read about Oracle Database and for new stuff to write about. An online recruiter would be completely useless to him . . . though related to his topic, still useless for his purpose.

Think about who will read your blog (your audience), and focus on things (products or services) that those people might be interested in. Think about this kind of thing before you even create a blog. Blogging about things like cars, even specific brands and models, is always interesting to someone, because lots of folks like particular brands or models of cars—so you know there's an audience. People who are into Jeeps, Land Rovers, or Range Rovers may well enjoy a blog such as this one:

www.ajeepthing.com/jeep-blog

This blog is run by Duane (yep, coauthor Duane). It is called Jeep, Land Rover, and Range Rover News and is independent of the manufacturers of Jeep and Land Rover. Duane's blog is likely to strike readers as being less biased than a blog run by Chrysler Corporation (which currently owns Jeep). Then again, some corporate blogs are respected as excellent communication tools with a reputation for honesty.

In the long run, blogging and financial success with your blog is often not about choosing a niche, or even getting people to read your blog. It's more about your talent to get people absorbed, your enthusiasm, and your persistence. Pick a topic that you like and that you know something about. It's going to take time. If you like it, you will be more likely to have the patience to persist. Above all, there is no one secret to success in any endeavor, as every successful entrepreneur is often successful for a different reason, and some even for a variety of reasons. In the case of blogging, you are trying to attract readers. You are trying to get them to return and to talk about your blog to other people. You also want them to say nice things, if possible. Make it interesting and compelling, and make sure you like doing it, because you might be at it for a very long time—and with very little response to begin with. Even then, with all these ingredients, there is no guarantee of success, but here are some more tips.

- *Technical stuff.* This is important because getting over the first hump of persuading people to notice your blog is the most difficult. Search engines, proper titling, labeling, keywords—this stuff is all important to get right. You are going to be at this for a while. For example, there are some indie musicians out there with some very appealing music. However, they will probably never even be heard. This is usually because they lack promotional, marketing, and sales skills. Lack of communication might keep even the most talented of artists in perpetual obscurity. Even record label Artist and Repertoire (A&R) people, the talent scouts of the music industry, will not go anywhere near bands or musicians who can't sell themselves. You can learn how to market yourself. Blogging is the same thing as any other marketing exercise. Get people to notice you, and the readers will come. It is possible to *learn* to write compelling content.

- *How many blogs?* You should probably start by hosting only one blog. If you want to run more than one, the costs could escalate quickly. You'll also need to account for the amount of time it takes to maintain a blog. Running multiple blogs requires all that time for every blog. After you get one up and running and have a good feel for what it takes to get a blog making money, you may well want to start other blogs on various topics.

TAPPING THE POWER OF LEADING BLOGS

Tapping into the power of the leading blogs is a process of using information in the most popular blogs to guide your activities. These types of Web sites can probably be vaguely divided into those that are social networks, those that provide personalized start pages, and those that are just blogs.

The problem with all of the social networking types of Web sites is that they are largely self-contained with respect to their user populations. Why? Those who run these sites don't want their users leaving. Additionally, a typically self-contained Web site of this nature is free to use blogs as well. Therefore, advertising is published by the owner of the Web site, not by bloggers or readers of *How to Make Money with Your Blog*. So, tapping into some hosted blogs, including those on social networks or free from hosting companies with your account, is really like giving them permission to place *their* ads on *your* content and letting them keep the revenues.

The best way for readers of *How to Make Money with Your Blog* to tap into the power of leading blogs is by reading those blogs, commenting, becoming involved, and telling people where they can find your blog. This is likely to be a time-consuming activity. Also, be careful not to irritate other bloggers by advertising yourself too directly on their blogs. Typically, blogging platforms allow a space for you to insert your own URL/domain (which links your username), so stick with that and allow folks to find you by clicking on your linked username. Well-thought-out responses and comments can garner a fair share of interest and traffic for you.

So, can you make use of the biggest blogs in order to attract traffic to your own blog? Yes, you can do this by becoming actively involved. Can you place ads on a profile on something such as a MySpace blog or on someone else's blog? No.

It comes down to how much time you can spend on this type of activity.

Social Network Blogging

MySpace is a self-contained social networking environment. This means that MySpace both controls and benefits from advertising revenue. This generally applies to all other social networking Web sites as well (YouTube, Friendster, Twitter, etc.).

Social networking Web sites are essentially free to use, but they must make revenue somehow. These Web sites make their revenue by publishing advertisements—just as you are trying to do with your blog. You could, of course, maintain one or more MySpace accounts and accounts on other social networking Web sites. You could use those accounts to attempt to drive traffic to your blog, where people will see *your* ads (not those published by MySpace). This would, however, be very time-consuming because a lot of active manual labor is required to maintain a presence on a social network. Essentially, you have to network yourself—you have to be an active MySpace user.

MySpace can be found at www.myspace.com, and YouTube is

at www.youtube.com. Other social networks include Friendster at www.friendster.com, Bebo at www.bebo.com, and Twitter at www.twitter.com. There are many other social networking sites, but their value is often in question. Expect some level of spam from these sites if you join. Wherever large groups of users congregate online, spammers are sure to follow. Well-established social networks like MySpace are fairly good at controlling irritating spam. YouTube simply does not contain the options that would allow mass marketers to target any specific market, so spam is less prevalent on YouTube than on MySpace. As with many things, your results may vary. The authors of this book are extremely selective about the social spaces they maintain. As Duane often says, "I don't need yet another place to maintain."

In general, it is unlikely that self-contained social networking blogs would be of much use to readers of *How to Make Money with Your Blog*—unless you have another reason for using a Web site like MySpace, such as being a musician, a comedian, or someone who is networking, professionally or personally.

Personalized Start Pages

Search engines such as Yahoo, Google, and Microsoft Network (MSN) have offered personalized start pages for many years. A personalized start page was originally intended as access to an online e-mail account whereby a user could add things like weather reports and news feeds. These pages have gradually grown into an amalgamation of all things offered by the search engines, including e-mail, personalization, blogging, and social networking profiles, among other things.

- *Yahoo 360.* This is another one of those Web sites that self-contains its users, and thus the advertising belongs to Yahoo and not the people who add the blog postings. In fact, the current implementation of Yahoo 360 looks very like a social networking Web site when one brings up the page in a browser. Essentially, Yahoo 360 is a simple extension to My Yahoo, including a blog, a spot for your pictures, and anything and everything else you might want to share about yourself. Yahoo 360 has its place in the world of the Internet, but not for a reader of *How to Make Money with Your Blog*. Yahoo 360 is a little like a personalized start page on steroids!

- *Google.* This is essentially the same offering as a Yahoo personalized start page, except it's from competing search engine Google. Google's blog facility is called Blogger and is the equivalent of Yahoo's Yahoo 360 blogging environment. Google's Blogger is more like a blog, containing much more flexibility for bloggers—like the ability to use your own ads. In the end, its limitations outweigh its usefulness.

- *MSN (Microsoft Network).* MSN is basically the same as Yahoo 360 and Google (plus Blogger), essentially being a storage repository for personal information, where the blog and the social networking profile allow users to make personal information public. Once again, advertising is self-contained and belongs to the MSN Web site.

Note: You can add any URL (Web site or blog) to your personalized start page on Yahoo, Google, and MSN.

Other Leading Blogs

Amazon Connect is an interesting blog system that allows for blogging and commentary by Amazon authors. An Amazon author is someone selling a book on the Amazon Web site. One disadvantage with Amazon Connect is that it doesn't send e-mails telling you when someone makes a comment. Perhaps this will change in the future. Amazon Connect is also not very user-friendly. For example, if you don't log on to Amazon Connect very often, the chances of remembering the password, or even the e-mail address you used to register, may be remote. It can take a day or two to get an e-mail through to the correct support person just to find the link to reset your password. Sometimes, software is written by techies, for techies—and can even be a challenge for a techie.

> Note: Software should be written for end users—easy to use; otherwise, people simply won't use it. Remember that when writing your blog. Write simply and clearly. Put yourself in the shoes of your readers and you will reach people more easily.

Gavin has around 15 titles published and available on Amazon, but he gets little response in his Amazon Connect blog. Any readers contacting him usually do so by e-mail.

The Entertainment Factor: Adding Multimedia to Your Blog

You can add multimedia to a blog, and there is much to be said for making online content more entertaining than just plain text. MySpace and YouTube are good examples of audio and video podcasting. MySpace started out as a musician's Web site, where musicians placed their audio content online as MP3s, and fans got to listen for free. YouTube goes a little further by offering video content from anyone to anyone. Some of the multimedia terms applying to blogging are as follows:

- *Podcasting*. This is broadcasting over the Internet using a feed consisting of audio, or video, or both. Typically, you download the feed and any updated shows. You can then listen to the content, or podcast, at any time you like. The term came from the explosive growth of the iPod and those offering unique content for people to load onto their iPods to listen to.

- *Audioblogging*. This is sharing of audio files over the Internet in a blog. MP3s are the most common format (for now), because they compress the most and lose little quality. MySpace allows musicians to upload MP3 files.

- *Photoblogging.* This is sharing of photographs by way of Internet blogs. Many social networks and blogging templates allow upload of photographs. Some Web sites are dedicated to sharing of photographs, with a security feature allowing you to keep sections private or enable them to be viewed by everyone. Many blog platforms also accommodate plug-ins to allow you to import your images into a dedicated space on your blog and showcase them as thumbnails.

- *Videoblogging.* This is sharing of video online. YouTube is the most popular example.

There is one problem with using multimedia in blogging. Adding too much multimedia to a blog can cause a serious problem for you. The average Internet user loses interest in a Web page and a Web site (your blog) in about seven seconds. If your content takes longer than seven seconds to load into a browser, then you lose people left, right, and center.

SUMMARY

Blogging really is primarily about targeting the right audience and then communicating with those people. Always try to keep the following tasks in mind while blogging:

- *Communicate.* Your readers are people. They are reading your blog. Communicate!

- *Keep people sweet.* You should express your opinion and encourage people to participate and express their opinions. Be emotional and passionate but don't go overboard and offend people.

- *Make use of blogspeak.* Fit in by speaking the language that other bloggers use. The old cliché, "When in Rome do as the Romans do," applies to blogging as well. If your chosen niche has its own jargon, use it as appropriate. It's often a good idea to have a glossary of terms developed and handy for those new to the topic, though. This is a nice touch that can make your blog stand out in the pack.

- *Blog successfully.* Be patient, persistent, and consistent. It takes time for the Internet to notice your new blog. Keep postings regular and make sure they're interesting. Most blogs are successful with niche audiences. There are far fewer mass-audience blogs, though successful ones do exist.

- *Use other Web sites.* You can make use of social networking Web sites such as MySpace and YouTube. However, you will be limited to communicating with people and won't be able to advertise directly. The advertising usually belongs to the companies running those Web sites.

- *Add multimedia wisely.* You can add any kind of multimedia to your blog, such as audio and video. Just be conscious of the download times for large multimedia objects. You have about seven seconds to capture someone's interest. Use the time wisely.

That's it! That's *How to Make Money with Your Blog.* We hope you have enjoyed reading this book as much as we've gotten a kick out of writing it. Go forth and use your newfound knowledge to make your blogging into a revenue generator for yourself—as well as a fun thing. Any updates on the art and science of *How to Make Money with Your Blog* can be found at Duane's online marketing blog:

www.theonlinemarketingguy.com

CONTACTING THE **AUTHORS**

Duane Forrester runs a number of blogs that accomplish just what this book is about: making money with blogs and blogging. Duane also frequently speaks all over North America. Duane can be contacted on the following e-mail addresses:

- searchgeek@gmail.com

- duane@theonlinemarketingguy.com

Duane runs the following blogs and Web sites:

- www.theonlinemarketingguy.com

- www.ajeepthing.com/jeep-blog

- www.blowupmyride.com

- www.dieseldiesel.com

Gavin Powell is an experienced computer technical writer with numerous titles in print, a software developer and administrator, and a semiprofessional composer and musician. Gavin also owns and administers various Web sites and blogs. Gavin can be contacted on the following e-mail addresses:

- ezpowel@ezpowell.com

- oracledba@oracledbaexpert.com

Gavin runs the following blogs, social networking profiles, and Web sites:

- ezpowellmusic.blogspot.com

- ezpowelltutorial.blogspot.com

- www.myspace.com/ezpowell

- www.youtube.com/ezpowell

- www.ezpowell.com

- www.oracledbaexpert.com

SOME OF THE WEB SITES **REFERENCED** IN THIS BOOK

Blogger (www.blogger.com)

BBlog (www.bblog.com)

SixApart (www.sixapart.com)

Greymatter
(www.noahgrey.com/greysoft)

Live Journal (www.livejournal.com)

20Six UK (www.20six.co.uk)

MindSay (www.mindsay.com)

Drupal (www.drupal.org)

HitTail (www.hittail.com)

Wordtracker (www.wordtracker.com)

KeyBoardDiscovery (www.keyworddiscovery.com)

To submit a blog or feed:

- www.getBlogs.com

- www.feedburner.com/fb/a/home

- www.Blogtopsites.com

- www.globeofBlogs.com

- www.technorati.com

- dir.Blogflux.com

- www.newsgator.com/Home.aspx

- www.Bloglines.com

- www.feedster.com/add.php

- www.Blogdex.net

- www.topix.net

- www.Blogwise.com

- www.boingboing.net

To announce a new post or article:

- rpc.pingomatic.com

- www.bblog.com/ping.php

- rpc.weblogs.com/RPC2

- www.ping.blo.gs

- rpc.technorati.com/rpc/ping

- xping.pubsub.com/ping
- ping.weblogalot.com/rpc.php
- pinger.blogflux.com/rpc
- rpc.pingomatic.com
- www.1470.net/api/ping
- api.feedster.com/ping
- api.feedster.com/ping.php
- api.moreover.com/ping
- api.moreover.com/RPC2
- api.my.yahoo.com/RPC2
- api.my.yahoo.com/rss/ping
- www.bblog.com/ping.php
- www.bitacoras.net/ping
- www.blogdb.jp/xmlrpc
- blog.goo.ne.jp/XMLRPC
- www.blogmatcher.com/u.php
- www.bulkfeeds.net/rpc
- www.coreblog.org/ping
- www.mod-pubsub.org/kn_apps/blogchatt
- ping.amagle.com
- ping.bitacoras.com
- ping.bloggers.jp/rpc
- ping.blogmura.jp/rpc

- ping.blo.gs
- ping.cocolog-nifty.com/xmlrpc
- pinger.blogflux.com/rpc
- ping.exblog.jp/xmlrpc
- ping.feedburner.com
- ping.myblog.jp
- pingqueue.com/rpc
- ping.blogg.de
- ping.rootblog.com/rpc.php
- ping.syndic8.com/xmlrpc.php
- ping.weblogalot.com/rpc.php
- ping.weblogs.se
- rcs.datashed.net/RPC2
- rpc.blogbuzzmachine.com/RPC2
- rpc.blogrolling.com/pinger
- rpc.britblog.com
- rpc.icerocket.com:10080
- rpc.newsgator.com
- rpc.pingomatic.com
- rpc.tailrank.com/feedburner/RPC2
- rpc.technorati.com/rpc/ping
- rpc.weblogs.com/RPC2
- rpc.wpkeys.com

- services.newsgator.com/ngws/xmlrpcping.aspx
- signup.alerts.msn.com/alerts-PREP/ submitPingExtended.doz
- topicexchange.com/RPC2
- trackback.bakeinu.jp/bakeping.php
- www.a2b.cc/setloc/bp.a2b
- www.bitacoles.net/ping.php
- www.blogdigger.com/RPC2
- www.blogoole.com/ping
- www.blogoon.net/ping
- www.blogpeople.net/servlet/weblogUpdates
- www.blogroots.com/tb_populi.blog?id=1
- www.blogshares.com/rpc.php
- www.blogsnow.com/ping
- www.blogstreet.com/xrbin/xmlrpc.cgi
- www.holycowdude.com/rpc/ping
- www.lasermemory.com/lsrpc
- www.imblogs.net/ping
- www.mod-pubsub.org/kn_apps/blogchatter/ping.php
- www.newsisfree.com/RPCCloud
- www.newsisfree.com/xmlrpctest.php
- www.popdex.com/addsite.php
- www.snipsnap.org/RPC2
- www.weblogues.com/RPC

- xmlrpc.blogg.de

- xping.pubsub.com/ping

- blogsearch.google.com/ping/RPC2

- rpc.technorati.com/rpc/ping

Here's a short list of contextual ad programs you should consider:

- Google AdSense (www.google.com/adsense)

- Yahoo Publisher Network (YPN) (publisher.yahoo.com)

- Clicksor (www.clicksor.com)

Here's a short list of ad networks you should consider:

- Blogads (www.Blogads.com)

- CrispAds (www.crispads.com)

- Blogsvertise (www.blogsvertise.com)

Two affiliate programs you might want to consider are as follows:

- Amazon.com
  (affiliate-program.amazon.com/gp/associates/join)

- Commission Junction (www.cj.com)

Some other affiliate programs are as follows:

- www.linkshare.com

- www.bidvertiser.com

- affiliates.ebay.com

Special thanks to those who helped with content in this book or offered their constructive feedback:

Bill Hartzer
www.billhartzer.com

Diane Vigil
www.dianev.com

Eric Ward
www.ericward.com

Lorelle VanFossen
lorelle.wordpress.com

Rose Sylvia
www.ppcthink.com

Chris Sherman
www.searchengineland.com

Vanessa Fox
www.vanessafoxnude.com (yes, it's work-safe)

INDEX